Art and Reality in the Novels of JOYCE CARY

Art and Reality in the Novels of JOYCE CARY

COLIN JOSEPH O'BRIEN

Commonwealth

Art and Reality in the Novels of Joyce Cary

Edition : 2020

ISBN 81-7169-076-9

Published by :
COMMONWEALTHPUBLISHERS
4831/24, Prahlad Street,
Ansari Road, Darya Ganj,
New Delhi - 110002
Ph. : 23275511, 23257835
e-mail : commonwealthbooks@gmail.com

Printed at :
Roshan Offset Printers
Delhi

PREFACE

The central concept is Joyce Cary's Novels is Reality which he himself enunciates in a primary document entitled *Art and Reality* given in his Clark Lectures. This dissertation aims at exemplifying Reality through a dozen novels of Cary, ten novels in the Carfax Edition and two published by Michael Joseph, London.

There are four major groups among the novels of Cary namely, four African novels, two childhool novels, three in the first trilogy and three in the second trilogy which present the complex of reality. Cary exemplifies mainly four types of Reality, primitive, imaginative, human and dogmatic.

Cary himself writes 'all great artists are preoccupied as if by nature, with reality. They assume from the beginning that it is their task to reveal a truth about some permanent and fundamental real'.[1] The novelist must develop a reality which is only there made actual, complete and purposeful to our experience'.[2] Joyce Cary develops this fundamental in his novels.

There are three differing views on Cary worked in different dissertations namely, *Joyce Cary : A Preface to his Novels* (1958) by Andrew Wright, *The Indeterminate World* (1962) by Robert Bloom and *The Dark Descent* (1965) by Golden Larsen. In addition to them there are several research papers on him such as in *Modern Fiction Studies, Autumn 1963*, Volume 9,

1. Joyce Cary : *Art and Reality* : *Ways of Creative Process*, Anchor Edn. (1958), p. 102.

2. *Ibid.*, p. 191.

No. 3. The conspectus of this thesis covers these, as also an evolving new point of view.

I express my gratitude to Late Dr. A.P. O'Brien, Retd. Professor and Head of the Department of English, Banaras Hindu University, Varanasi, who posed the problem and lay out. My gratefullness to Dr. Q.M. Khan, Reader in English, Ravenshaw College, Cuttack, for guiding me throughout my research. I am thankful to the British Council and friends in the United States for sending me the three dissertations on Cary.

Colin Joseph O'Brien

CONTENTS

CHAPTER I

An Historical Survey

The history of the English novel and its literary tradition, different from that of the American novel, is primarily sociological in character. Society was accepted as the basis of the novelist's are and the source of his creation. The trend from Defoe to Hardy 'has been man in society and society in the totality, on organism which has been examined with varying degrees of acuteness and emphasis as taste and fashion in the novel has ebbed and flowed'.[1] Fielding gave a plane mirror reflection of society, of the boisterous side of life, in *Joseph Andrews* or *Tom Jones*. Defoe's chronicle Moll Planders deals with a woman of vulgarity, but the judgment of the author rests on the social sanction of her times :

> ......there is not a wicked action in any part of it, but is first or last rendered unhappy and unfortunate ; there is not a superlative villain brought upon the stage, but either he is brought to an unhappy end, or brought to be a paintent ; there is not an ill thing mentioned but it is condemned, even in the relation, nor a virtuous, just thing but it carries its praise along with it.[2]

Jane Austen dealt with social comedy, with money and marriage in the quiet countryside. She described society largely in equilibrium.[3] The creative vitality and vigour of

1. John McCormick, *Catastrophe and Imagination* (London, 1957), p. 3.
2. Defoe, Author's Preface, Moll Flanders (Boston, 1903), I, xix-xx.
3. Joseph Warren Beach, *English Literature of the 19th and the early 20th Centuries, 1798 to the First World War* (New York, 1962), p. 79.

whiteman, well intentioned, tries to lift the Birri tribe ; he is martyred by the insensate natives. Marie Hasluck, an anthropologist, is the American visitor, who takes a romantic view of the Birri ; she is soon disillusioned. She marries Bewsher and suffers to see him die. Bewsher's death is differently received by the characters each in the bias of his life. The African Witch (1936) is replete with demonology. The African native Aladai, educated at Oxford, is subdued by his sister Elizabeth the priestess with magical powers. The *ju-ju* spirit is symbolizes in that creature of terror the crocodile. In *Mister Johnson* (1939), a youth of seventeen is obssessed with civilised life. He takes part in the building of a road which stands as a symbol of western progress. Johnson helps Rudbeck, but is caught in crime. He is sentenced to death but before that takes place Rudbeck shoots him. All four African novels, with their own slants of truth, deal with primitive reality.

In the two novels of *Charley is My Darling* (1940) and *A House of Children* (1941) Cary is concerned with imaginative reality. The child is in continuous process of building and ordered world from fragmentary. In *Charley is My Darling* crime is considered as a moral experiment. The story is one of adjustment and disaster. The novel *A House of Children* is written with lyrical fervour. It gives a romantic view of childhood with its mingling of the sensory and the imaginative.

The first trilogy presents human reality. The three novels deal with the chaos of live and the universal within it. *In Herself Surprised* (1941). Sara, the broken woman, turns on herself to the goodness that could be possible but which is not hers. In *To be a Pilgrim* (1942) we are shown three generations. The characters form two groups, the aberrants and the constants, those in the unreal and those in the real. *The Horse's Mouth* (1944) is the last novel in the group. It deals with the life of Gulley Jimson, the Wayward artist, whose *The Fall* is put to rude use for patching the roof of Mrs. Coker and *The Creation* in the drawing of which Gulley Jimson suffers a fall. This comedy is a triumph of laughter, what happens to a soldier, just before he goes out to no-man's land and death.

Dogmatic Reality is of two kinds that which is based on a system of sanctioned dogmas in a religion and that which is privately evolved. As the first deals with the transcendental and Absolute Reality, outside the mind, the second deals with Relative Reality. *Prisoner of Grace* (1952) is shown as dealing with relativism of dogmatic Reality, *Except the Lord* (1953) with moral absolutism or dogma in Envangelical christainity and *Not Honour More* (1955) with the ultimate perceived by a character, Jim Latter in particular moments of his life.

The art of Joyce Cary moves from intuition to concept. Each novel is occasioned by a intuition or discovery, or an impression or some passing thought usually expressed in the prefatory Essay of the novel where one such exists. As the novel evolves and human beings work out their destinies as free souls, they find themselves facing the changeless and the permanent. All works of art, once wrote Cary, 'exist and must exist within a universal moral real' (Art and Reality). This is the Reality, multiform in its very nature, which Cary dissects and presents, in striking differentiation and selective proportions. To explain and expound the novels from this point of view has been the burden of this thesis.

Introduction

Joyce Cary (1888-1957) wrote his first novel *Aissa Saved* in 1932 and *Not Honour More* in 1955, the splendid climax of fifteen novels. His sixteenth *The Captive and the Free*, unfinished, was completed by Winifred Davin, literary Adviser to the estate of Joyce Cary. Even such an original writer, as Cary was, has to be perceptually seen in the tradition of the English novel. He is in the tide of the continuity of the modern novel Cary is inimitable and amazingly unique. He is a challenging novelist and it takes courage to take up the gauntlet. It was done by three bold critics. The first is Andrew Wright : *Joyce Cary* : A Preface to his Novels (1958) who finds in him the theme of freedom. The second is Robert Bloom : *The Indeterminate World* (1962) who find Cary a disquieting indeterminate vision which impairs his novels. The third is Golden Larsen : *The Dark Descent* : *Social Change and Moral Responsibility in the Novels of Joyce Cary* (1965). The approach is explicit in the sub-title. None of these appear to be centric to Cary's Art. He ruminated on Art and the Artist and embodied his view in his Clark Lectures published under thet itle *Art and Reality* : *Ways of Creative Process* (1958). Cary's primary purpose was to present the complex of Reality, the stance taken in this thesis.

The first group of four African novels deal with instinctive life and primodial images they are within the study of anthropology or dark reality as it appears in primitive consciousness. *In Aissa Saved* (1932) he studies primitive life at the group level. The African Characters live in superstition and barbarism. The christain convert Aissa succumbs to the overpowering and immutable laws of Race. The whole story throbs with jungle fear and foreboding. In *An American Visitor* (1933) Bewsher, the

Thackeray was directed to society rather than to a character. *Vanity Fair* is a novel without a hero in the traditional sense—a novel of social pretence and vanity in society. Even 'romanticism faltered at social fact'.[4] Scott who wrote romantic novels related them to ordinary human events in the common mode of perception of the nineteenth century novelists.

There were certain clearly defined values or norms in society by which the individual was governed and judged. The character in the novel, in spite of his bitter personal reactions which he at times showed against the social order, could never challenge its values and would ultimately realize that the only sensible course open to him was to get reconciled to them. Erring characters were held up to ridicule, divested of their delusions and finally made to behave in conformity with the codes and conventions that ensured social stability. This is the theme of *Pride and Prejudice* and *Emma.* The social behaviour of man was more important than the man himself with his personal notions and feelings. The emergence of the middle class between 1750 and 1850 was significant ; it determined the nature of the novel which had to cater to the taste of this great and dominating class.[5] This community did not show the least interest in the abstruse philosophies of Kant or Hegel which informed the German novel generally, but considered Bentham, who propounded utilitarianism, the genuins of the age.[6] The novelists who drew their characters from the middle class could not explore their minds in depth. As David Cecil observes :

> The limitation of subject matter limits in its turn their range of characters, their most successful creations, Mr. Micawber, Becky Sharp, Mrs. Proudie, Madam Beck, are all what actors call "character parts", marked individual types whose interest lies in their comic or picturesque

4. John Loofbourow, *Thackeray and the Form of Fiction* (Princeton, New Jersey, 1964), p. 51.

5. David Cecil, *Early Victorian Novelists*, (London, 1935), p. 18.

6. John McCormick, *op. cit.*, p. 8.

> idiosyncrasy of speech and manner rather than in their relation to any general problems or interests of human nature. They are of the family of the Aguecheeks and Dame Quicklys ; there are no Hamlets among them ; no intellectuals, statesmen, or artists. For those deeper issues of human life which are the main interests of such characters do not form any part of the Victorian subject matter.[7]

Dickens presents in *Great Expectations* the deep yearning of the progressive middle class for greater prosperity under the influence of Bentham's utilitarianism. Dickens was mainly concerned with the injustices, cruelties and the exploitation of the day and created a number of types through which he ridiculed the deviations of people from the path of righteousness. He sought to arouse the social conscience through his art. The middle class society gradually making its way into the moneyed circles figures prominently in the novels of Thackeray. Trollope's *Orley Farm* fully represents the class structure of the victorian society which includes the Lords and Ladies, the business community and the lower classes. Trollope had a clear insight into the moral implications of the social behaviour of his characters. George Eliot is the only novelist who created individuals engaged in resolving their moral dilemmas arising out of social situation in which they are placed. They are 'recognizably true to life' and present 'the nuances of class distinction'.[8] With Hardy, who is regarded as the last of the victorian novelists, the novel takes a turn. While the earlier Victorian novelists fully recognized the importance of social stability for individual progress, Hardy brings out the conflict between individual will and social convention. Frederick R. Karl defines the new hero in Hardy's fiction :

> The century that began with Jane Austen's well-balanced heroines of strong will, who literally "will" them-

7. David Cecil, *op. cit.*, p. 9.
8. Walter Allen, *The English Novel*, Penguin Books (Reprinted, 1963), p. 179.

selves into normal behaviour, rushes towards its end with the willful self-destructiveness of Hardy's heroines and heroes who "will" themselves not into normality but into an obsession with guilt and penance.[9]

Chance in Hardy's novels is a fitting antithesis to the set pattern of social beliefs. Hardy's hero is under the pressure of some inscrutable power that works out his doom. Man's immediate problems, when considered against this background, seem insignificant and trivial. Man is a puny figure compared to his natural surroundings, the impersonal forces of the vast cosmic reality which surrounds him. Aware of these he still sets himself against and in defiance of social restrictions. Hardy succeeds in crystallising individual alienation from society in an aesthetically satisfying form, no matter how unsatisfying is the ethical content of a malignant or indifferent God or "President of the immortals".

Towards the beginning of the twentieth century the social framework came in for criticism. World War I toppled down the edifice of Victorian morality and social complacency. The well-defined synthetic approach of the Victorians resulted in a confusion of values and social fragmentation. Walter Allen described this disintegration with valid elaboration and in expressive Language :

> The war split the landscape of time like an enormous natural catastrophe, obliterating long-established boundaries, blowing sky-high landmarks that for years had been taken for granted. It lay like an unbridgeable chasm between the present and the past, so that present and past seemed almost laughably different in kind. It set a gulf between the young who had fought it and the old who had stayed at home. What had seemed certainties, all the assumptions nurtured in Britain by a hundred years of virtual peace, during which

9. Frederick R. Karl, "The Mayor of Casterbridge ; A New Fiction Defined, *Modern British Fiction*, ed., Mark Schorer (New York, 1961), p. 10.

> wars were fought either by foreigners or, if the British were involved, by small professional armies on the peripheries of empire, were exposed as illusions. The war had speeded up social change as it had never been speeded up before. It emancipated women ; it emancipated the working class. It made the motor-car and the aeroplane common place. It affected everything and everybody. Nothing was as it was before.[10]

Social values were no longer taken for granted. Those who departed from social standards and codes were no longer the butt of satire or ridicule. There was a shift from social comedy to personal tragedy. Plot was subordinated to the psychological exploration of character. The novel of manners gave place to the novel of alienation. The Victorian novelists always kept in view the social pattern. Old social conventions crumbled down and there was a new awareness of some change in the social fabric. The novel took a new turn. While society formed the background, the hero is at odds with the environment. Hardy's characters are in perpetual conflict with society. The individual becomes supreme and society remains as a negative force. The conventionally plotted novel saw its end. The centre of the drama of human life is shifted from society to the individual. Hardy's characters defy the rules of sexual conduct prescribed by society and stand apart as isolated heroes or heroines. There is no social sanction behind them or their deeds.

The nineteenth century novelist strove to adjust the individual psychology, behaviour and beliefs to the social climate within which he lived. The increasing complexity of social problems brought a corresponding change in the form of the novel. The novel before 1910 could be written on the conventional pattern. Plot and character were structural essentials and events were arranged in a chronological sequence and led to a logical conclusion. The novelist strictly followed the rules of exposition, complication and resolution.

10. Walter Allen, *Tradition and Dream*, Penguin Books (1965), p. 25.

With the draw of the twentieth century the conventional aesthetics proved too feeble and simplified a technique for the presentation of baffling realities. Civilization was breaking down under the impact of diverse forces, such as the progress of science, the First World War and the social and economic revolutions of 1914-25.[11] There was a universal catastrophe which affected sensibility and deepened the dichotomy of the self from society. John McCormick commenting on the effect of World War I actually summarized the situation when he wrote :

> The catastrophe brought into modern society a sense of urgency and a new tempo ; it made for a new consciousness of self and of the place of self in society ; it created an atmosphere in which the loss of old certainties, the presence of new anxieties, and the thrusting forward of public issues combined to isolate man from man and group from group.[12]

New techniques were evolved to depict the complex phenomena. Experiments were made. Virginia Woolf envisaged a new kind of novel as a dramatic lyric :

> Why not invent a new kind of play......Away from facts ; free ; yet concentrated ; prose yet poetry ; a novel and a play.[13]

She wove rhythmic patterns of language and poetic images into the texture of her novels. Mr. Dalloway sewing by the window is typical :

> Quiet descended on her, calm, content, as her needle drawing the silk smoothly to its gentle pause, collected the green folds together, and attached them very lightly to the

11. John McCormic, *op. cit.*, p. 38.

12. *Ibid.*, *p.* 41.

13. Virginia Woolf, *A Writer's Diary*, ed., Leonard Woolf (London, 1953), pp. 104-5.

belt. So, on a summer's day, waves collect, overballance and fall ; collect and fall ; and the whole world seems to be saying, that is all, more and more ponderously, until even the heart in the body which lies in the sun on the beach, says too, that is all. Fear no more, says the heart. Fear no more says the heart, committing its burthen to some sea which sighs collectively for all sorrows, and renews, begins, collects, lets fall. And the body alone listens to the passing bee.[14]

Now the individual mind having engaged the novelist's attention, the stream-of-consciousness technique proved an effective medium for the novelist, for the novelist could now concentrate on the exploration of 'pre-speech levels of consciousness for the purpose, primarily, of revealing the psychic being of his characters'.[15] Unlike the naturalist's taste for photographic details, the stream-of-consciousness writer was concerned with reality on the psychological plane. The technique was significant. The reader could have a direct rapport with the character and probe into his mind without being in the least aware of the writer's manipulative presence, a fact which distinguishes the modern novel from the Victorian novel where the novelist's repeated intrusion is almost irritating and dissolves the illusion of reality. The technique, moreover, provided a new means to the novelist to examine society through a prism or the radiant consciousness of the living mind.

There was a liberation of the individual sensibility from external life or schemata as found in the novels of Wells, Bennett and Galsworthy. Virginia Woolf described the new technique and its manifold involutions in a remarkable passage which brings out what Henry James calls 'each seized identify' :

---

14. Virginia Woolf, *Mrs. Dalloway*, Penguin Books (1964), pp. 44-5.

15. Robert Humphrey, Stream of Consciousness in the *Modern Novel* (Berkeley, 1954), p. 2.

> Examine for a moment an ordinary mind on an ordinary day. The mind receives a myriad impressions—trivial, fantastic, evanescent, or ingraved with the sharpness of steel. From all sides they come, an incessant shower of innumerable atoms, and as they fall, as they shape themselves into the life of Monday or Tuesday, the accent falls differently from of old; the moment of importance came not here but there ; so that, if the writer were a free man and not a slave, if he could base his work upon his own feeling and not upon convention, there would be no plot, no comedy, no tragedy, and no love interest or catastrophe in the accepted style.[16]

The traditional approach to reveal character in action, speech or manners was discarded by woolf. She pre-empted for action presented not lineally but spatially, concerned with the growth of consciousness. Action is developed to the extent that it necessitates the presence of a character at a particular time and place for fictional reality. The psychic make-up or the complex personality of the character is intimately bound up with events in the past rather than with action in the present external surroundings. The character is best understood in terms of what he has been in the past rather than what he is in the present. Retrospective analysis enlightens the present more than a realistic assessment of the immediate situations would do. The real self is revealed in the past. The mind stumbles on an immediate object that sets in motion a chain of associations or disjointed flows of consciousness that link the present to the past. The pattern emerges out of the flux of experience and impressions. Sociological reality gives place to points of illumination in the inner life.

One of the characteristics of the modern novel is the isolation of the protagonist. He feels himself alone in a hostile surrounding like Hardy's Henchard cut off from his townsmen. He 'is in some ways the English prototype of the Twentieth

16. Virginia Woolf, "Modern Fiction", *English Critical Essays—Twentieth Century* (London, 1958), p. 393.

Century's insolated hero, the dominating figure in a world suddenly inexplicable by human reason'.[17] Allen Tate writes that one great subject of the modern novel is 'a man alone in society or even against society, almost never with society'.[18] In the novels of Conrad and D.H. Lawrence there was a shift of emphasis from the outer world to individual human experience. Insolated from his fellows, the hero struggles towards individual selfhood. In Conrad's Novels, however lonely the character, he is ultimately conscious of the moral imperative of his existence. There is an instinctive awareness of the individual conscience. As Morton D. Zabel comments :

> The measure of Conrad's character and his artistry may be taken from the fact that neither his sense of honour nor his sense of realism permitted him to betray the conscience which it took him half his life to discover in himself, and the other half to test and dramatize in his books.[19]

In *Lord Jim* the single figure of Jim is the ethical and emotional centre of himself and of everything around : all the other characters and events exist simply to reveal some aspect of the configuration of his soul. At the centre of Conrad's fiction is the utter sense of loneliness. 'His vision of man', writes Elizabeth Drew, 'shapes itself so often into the drama of some exile, some man without a country, some outcast, some lonely sea captain, someone in the grip of solitary struggle.... our interest is centered in one human personality and his fate. Not the malignant irony of external events, but the moral and emotional quality of man's response to them is Conrad's theme'.[20]

---

17. Frederick R. Karl, *op. cit.*, p. 28.

18. Allen Tate, "Techniques of Fiction", *Forms of Modern Fiction*, ed., William Van O'Connor (Bloomington, 1961), p. 43.

19. Morton D. Zabel, "Chance and Recognition", *Modern British Fiction*, ed., Mark Schorer (New York, 1961), p. 83.

20. Elizabeth Drew, *The Novel : A Modern Guide to Fifteen English Masterpieces* (New York, 1963), p. 158.

The crisis in almost everyone of Conrad's novels arises when, by accident, or an act of decision or error emanating from peculiar inner urges or psychological compulsions, the central character finds himself abruptly committed to his destiny. He is faced with moral dilemmas, within and without himself, his betrayal of the community and his final acceptance of the same. This emphasis within the character does not exclude the events or the total reality in which the character exists. F.R. Leavis writes of this :

> Conrad's study of motives, and of the relation between the material and spiritual, doesn't depend for its impressiveness on any sustained analytic exhibition of the inner complexities of the individual psyche. The impressiveness lies in the vivid reality of the things we are made to see and hear, and the significance they get from their relations in a highly organized and vividly realized whole.[21]

The stress, thus, in the modern novel is on the individual, his moral responsibility, and the awareness of a larger reality.

Like Conrad, D.H. Lawrence dealt with the individual but another place of realized life. As against the merging of the past and the present in the flow of individual consciousness depicted by experimental novelists like Virginia Woolf, Lawrence creates complex characters trying to understand their own 'dark soul' in the age conditioned by mechanical contrivances. Lawrence stands for uninhibited life unconfined to a predetermined, conventional moral scheme. He had enunciated his basic view in 1912 in significant passage :

> My great religion is a belief in the blood, the flesh, as being wiser than the intellect. We can go wrong in our minds. But what the blood feels, and believes, and says, is always true.[22]

He was for instinctive life and a pattern conceived as psychic

21. F.R. Leavis, *The Great Tradition*, Penguin Books (1962), p. 217.
22. *Letters of D.H. Lawrence*, ed., Aldous Huxley (London, 1952), p. xiv,

drama. He knew 'that for fulfilment man must live from deeper sources than the purely conscious surface of the mind and he awakens and reveals these'.[23]

The social environments that pervert the spontaneous life act as negative forces. He was aware of society in a deterministic technological civilization. Critical of this he wrote :

> Assert purposiveness as the one supreme and pure activity of life, and you drift into barren sterility, like our business life of today, and our political life, you become sterile, you make anarchy inevitable.[24]

The Rainbow is the only English novel which recorded society and the individual as transverse to it. It presents, as Marvin Mudrick writes, 'the social revolution whereby Western man lost his sense of community and men—more especially, women—learned, if they could, that there is no help any longer except in the individual and in his capacity for a passional life'.[25] He found life sacrificed to 'coal and iron', and ugliness, the background of *Sons and Lovers* and the final version of *Lady Chatterley's Lover* in the description of the motor trip trough Derbyshire.

Lawrence as a novelist captures the moment of life itself, both in men and women in the physical world of nature and the 'circumambient universe'. He is concerned with finer shades like the quality of experience and the depth of the individual human being's response to experience. This accounts for his duality of perceptions. He called, for example, Italians, 'Children of the Sun' and at the same time found their souls 'dark and nocturnal'.[26] What preoccupied him was not social man or the 'societal being' but, as Walter Allen writes, 'the seven-

23. Elizabeth Drew, *op. cit.*, p. 223.

24. D.H. Lawrence, *Fantasia of the Unconscious*, p. 108.

25. Marvin Murdick, "The Originality of *The Rainbow*", *Modern British Fiction*, ed., Mark Schorer (New York, 1961), p. 250.

26. D.H. Lawrence, *Twilight in Italy*, p. 32.

eights of the iceberg of personality submerged and never seen, the unconscious mind'.[27]

Virginia Woolf, Conrad and D.H. Lawrence indicate a significant trend of the modern novel. From them to Aldous Huxley and Graham Greene is a step into a different province of art. There is a disappearance from the familiar 'Conceptual Hero' or 'the focal character of the classical novel'.[28] Instead there is, as O'Faolain terms it, the 'Anti-Hero' concept.[29] With the gradual fading away of traditional certainties, the Hero is a lost soul crying out for definite values. The outline of the character is not definite as that of the 'Conceptual Hero' but appears inchoate in the flux of life 'groping, puzzled, cross, mocking, frustrated and isolated, manfully or blunderingly trying to establish his own personal, supra-social codes'.[30]

Aldous Huxiey's novels, particularly the early ones, are novels of ideas or the intellectualization of characters. The human personality is attenuated into an aspect so that characters in conflict or in association indicate a series of arguments in progress, arguments fluctuating between the logical or the specious, the rational and the platitudinous. The morbidly exacting critic, as Aldous Huxley is, moves with the novel. The dialogue of a noval is carried over waves of ideas, moving forward and backward like the waves of the sea breaking on the beach and returning back to the sea. In *Point Counter Point*, the conversation is on old age and it runs :

The old really are n't possible....It's no good ; you can't have any dealings with them.

Spandrell laughed, "You speak of the old as though they were Kaffirs or Eskimos".

---

27. Walter Allen, *The English Novel*, Penguin Books (Reprinted 1963) pp. 361-2.
28. Seen O'Faolain, *The Varnishing Hero* (London, 1956), p. 14.
29. *Ibid.*, p. 16.
30. *Ibid.*, p. 17.

Well, isn't that just about what they are? Hearts of gold and all that. And wonderfully intelligent—in their own way, and all things considered. But they don't happen to belong to our civilization. They're aliens....Old people always remind me of an Arab tea party. Do you suppose we shall be an Arab tea party when we're old?

Yes, and probably a death's head into the bargain, said Spandrell. "It's a question of thickening arteries".[31]

Even within the single character there is a fissure of ideas, a kind of schizophrenia. In *Those Barren Leaves* Mrs. Aldwinkle thinks of her high level of art and at the same time is entrenched in a money-making racket. She speaks to Irene, her niece :

Art's the great thing, Mrs. Aldwinkle was saying earnestly, "the thing that really matters, makes life worth living and justifies one's existence....It's the highest life.... It's the only life".

But she employed an arrey of means and persons to a mass money for her :

....at this very moment, men and women of every race and colour were doing their bit to supply Mrs. Aldwinkle with her income. On the two hundred and seventy thousand pounds of Mrs. Aldwinkle's capital the sun never sets ; She for art only, they—albeit unconscious of the privilege—for art in her.[32]

The novel of ideas is basic to Aldous Huxley. But the novel, by its nature and genre, deals with the emotional representation of life. Aware of this finer effect and points of illumination in

31. Aldous Huxley, *Point Counter Point*, Penguin Books (Reprinted 1965), pp. 137-8.

32. Aldous Huxley, *Those Barren Leaves*, Penguin Books (Reprinted 1961), pp. 55-6.

individual characters and human relations, Philip Quarles in *Point Counter Point* records in his note :

> Novel of ideas. The character of each personage must be implied, so far as possible, in the ideas of which he is the mouthpiece. In so far as theories are rationalisations of sentiments, instincts, dispositions of soul, this is feasible. The chief defect of the novel of ideas is that you must write about people who have ideas to express—which excludes all but about .01 per cent of the human race. Hence the real, congenital novelists do not write such books. But then I have never pretended to be a congenital novelist.[33]

It is interesting to consider one of Huxley's novels. *The Genuis and the Goddess* where 'sentiments, instinct, disoppositions of the soul' matter and are rationalized. This is the story of Dr. Henry Maartens, 'the genuis', a professor of physics, Kate, his wife, the goddess', and John Rivers who is involved in a complex love issue for both Kate and her daughter, Ruth, are in love with him. The narrative ends with the deaths [illegible] Kate and Ruth in a motor accident. The novel's huma[illegible] passional aspects are well depicted, but they are the undertones ; the major aspect is the idealogical interpretation neatly and intellectually formulated in different parts of the novel, such as, 'the criterion of reality is its intrinsic irrelevance',[34] or, further on towards the end of the novel, there are two kinds of Predestination. The Predestination of events, and at the same time the Predestination of two temperaments'.[35]

The disillusionment with contemporary civilization drove huxley to create type characters largely, in the grip of agony and frustration for lack of the positive values that nurtured the society of the past. They are no better than automatons speaking out the ideas of the author. They are for removed from the

---

33. Aldous Huxley, *op. cit*, p. 299.
34. Aldox Huxley, *The Genius and The Goddess* (London, 1955), p.7.
35. *Ibid.*, p. 124.

dramatic tension arising from tangible human relations. The 'Conceptual Hero' ultimately reconciled to his human surroundings does not figure in Huxley's world, a world framed within an assemblage of ideas. Huxley's interest for us 'lies in his being such a perfect representative of an angry and disoriented' age.[36]

Both Aldous Huxley and Graham Greene do not reveal the traditional hero or a prescribed scheme of life in an ordered society. The whiskey priest in Greene's *The Power and the Glory* is an anti-hero. He is a Roman Catholic priest different from priests. He is lewd ; he drinks ; he has broken his vows of chastity and obedience ; his sacerdotal office is abused. He is not close to the tabernacle light in a church, or a blaze of the candles and the ritual of worship. So powerfully brought out by Evenlyn Waugh in *Brideshead Revisited.* Burdened with guilt and sin, Greene's whiskey priest is bounded by the police through the malaria infested forests of Mexico. He is arrested, imprisoned, sentenced to death and is shot. He makes a broken confession his death and in that gets salvation. The motif of the novel is not the human story but the quasi-theological idea how eternity lies even next door to evanescent Time, and salvation at the very edge of damnation.

Greene deals with the choas of human life even at its extreme terminable end—dark despair. In *The Heart of the Matter* scobbie, the Deputy Commissioner in West Africa, loved no one, not even God and did the unforgivable act on his own life, committed suicide. In every way a non-conformist and an anarchist, he does not belong to the humanist tradition of beliefs and ideals or the religious humanism found in the novels of George Eliot. Scobbie, too, is saved as startingly expressed by Father Rank. The ambiguity of life is given in paradoxes, *e.g.*, 'only the man of good will carries always in his heart this capacity for damnation'.[37] The subletly of the ideas in the

36. Seen O' Faolain, *op. cit.*, p. 39

37. Graham Green, *The Heart of the Matter* (London, 1948), p. 60.

complex of evils makes this novel, like *The end of the Affair. The Quiet American, The Burn.-Out Case*, abnormal studies not in the realm of psychology but in the centralized view of the evil life and the transcendental life held by the novelist. Notwithstanding the depth of the themes in Greene, his art-form appears manipulated. He reduced man's statute and impugned his free will, making ultimately 'his people so subservient to his theme that they become its puppets'.[38]

The English novel has moved along different, well-marked and specific levels. In the nineteenth century and the Victorian era, there was the conceptual hero pattern of the individual in an ordered society and an accepted humanist tradition. From Fielding to Thackeray, with variants, human relations were conceived, relevant to norms of conduct or a pragmatic view of life derived from society and established conventions. In the twentieth century the ordered pattern broke up. There was a fift between the individual and society leading to the isolation of the hero in tragic loneliness in the novels of Thomas Hardy, or involved in inwardness or the stream of consciousness in the novels of Virginia Woolf or in the depths of conscience in the novels of Joseph Conrad. With the disintegration which overlook civilization in the twentieth century with World War First and later in World War Second, the novel developed the anti-Hero concept. The character was not wholly a human personality ; it received meaning and significance from the writer's centralized concept. Aldous Huxley wrote novels of ideas which emasculated sentiments and emotions in character and made them figures in a game of chess manipulated by the novelist himself. Graham Greene created characters not in relation to the proverbial human density of marriage, domestic happiness or social pieties. He gives 'no solution of a purely human nature' but expounds an ultimate destiny for man in the Hereafter. Both Huxley and Greene show heroes in the coherence or incoherence of life, each made to exemplify the novelist's predetermined concepts.

38. Sean O'Faolain, *op. cit.*, p. 91.

These changes in the history of the novel are essential as a backdrop for a study of Joyce Cary. His innovations get meaning from what obtained in the novel of the past or what changes took place in the novel of the present up to his emergence. Cary was a complex novelist in whom we find a forest of tangles, in theme and form, some of which, when isolated, have a historical continuation with some trend of the novel, or a discontinuation from what was ever written of the isolated hero or the anti-hero.

Cary's world is vast and seemingly inchoate. He wrote Prefaces, a book of Aesthetics, *Art and* Reality, fifteen novels, some of them massive on their own, or correlated with his other novels. The total output is a bewildering mass of multiple characters and events and a myriad reflections in a creative world of vast boundaries. To the critic he is a challenging novelist. The data are vast, the inferences many. Can there be any sense or a centralized view of him? If so, what are the referentials which will give or make sense without destroying the creative greatness of his genius?

There are, besides the several research papers on Cary, three major works which attempted an organized or full-length study of the novelist. The first is *Joyce Cary, A Preface to his Novels* by Andrew Wright (1958). This book has been written at a great advantage had has an unusual amount of authenticity. Andrew Wright stayed with Cary at Parks Road, Oxford, for six months and got access to the manuscripts of the novels, the short stories, essays, plays, poems, journals, letters and memoranda.[39] He witnessed the vast amount of work that Cary put into his novels. Chapters were transposed from one place to another, novels were cut down from 300,000 words to 100,000 words. Andrew Wright records Cary's statement on this 'fearful waste': 'I have tried to avoid it, but it

39. Andrew Wright, *Joyce Cary: A Preface to his Novels* (London, 1959), pp. 7-8.

seems to me the only way in which I can get the kind of form, I want, a certain balance and unity within a given context'.[40]

The book embodies some of the insights which Cary communicated to him. He takes the author's point of view but realizes that the writer is not always the best judge of his works. He, therefore, tries to give his critical estimate of the novelist. He emphasizes 'the primacy of theme' in Cary which he finds to be the freedom of man. He explores 'freedom's shape and freedom's consequences'[41] though all the novels. The dominant theme, according to Wright, is Cary's fascination for the free soul. But Wright ignores an important essential, namely, the objective absolute in which the individual is placed. Wright wrote his book early in 1958 and was deprived of Cary's theory of aesthetics, *Art and Reality*, which was published later in the year.

The second important book on Cary is Robert Bloom's *The Indeterminate World : A Study of the Novels* of Joyce Cary (1962). In Bloom's dissertation he accuses Cary of failing to impose a meaningful shape on his fiction. He finds Cary's characters living in a world of their own private beliefs which have nothing to do with the reality around. He estimates Cary's concept of reality as purely subjective in the case of each character and his 'doctrine of private world becomes a way of avoiding real commitment to particular private world. Cary tends to rest content with an account of the possibilities of diverse belief, so that his outlook is implicitly relativistic'.[42] Bloom is critical of Cary's 'consistent exaltation of individual character and personality as the primary locus of reality and unity in the world'.[43] He, thus, finds that Cary's world is indeterminate.

40. *Ibid.*, p. 15.

41. *Ibid.*, p. 28.

42. Robert Bloom, *The Indeterminate World : Study of the Novels of Joyce Cary* (Philadelphia, 1962), p. 8.

43. *Ibid.*, p. 43.

Bloom's whole approach is largely pejorative. He confines himself to a limited view of the novels themselves. There is undoubtedly the vast chaos of human experience and the private world of the individuals. But they are related to the universal or some absolutes. The illogicality and absurdity in the characters can be measured against the norms which appear in the context of a 'total relevance'. This is the basic kind of organization in the novels and which accounts for their dramatic existence. There are two perceptive worlds in Cary, an indeterminate world, and, a very much so, determinate world.

The third major work is Golden Larsen's *The Dark Descent: Social Change and Moral Responsibility in the Novels of Joyce Cary* (1965). Larsen's contention is that the individual and society are the two correlations which best expound the vision of Joyce Cary. He considers the individual as being and becoming and society in a continual state of revolution and change. He illustrates this from the African novels and the first trilogy primarily. He points out that account of social confusion the individual character is involved 'in a crisis of shifting values'.[44] Larsen is rather summary in his study of the second trilogy. *The Dark Descent* signifies the complete moral degeneration of an individual in a confused society which is in a state of flux and change.

Larsen's thesis deals with the 'play of opposing ideas'—the individual and society. These are evinced in the novels but there are more in them than just these. The Prefaces and the Clark Lectures, *Art and Reality*, consider these items but go beyond that to major pronouncements on the complex of Reality towards which the novelist strives in a number of apprehensions given in the stories or the diversity of characters in the Gothic and bizarre patterns of life. The object of this thesis is to show the encounter of individuals in a society which hardly receives them and Universals. Joyce Cary admits

---

44. Golden L. Larsen, *The Dark Descent: Social Change and Moral Responsibility in the Novels of Joyce Cary* (London, 1965), p. 20.

Reality. It is in life and human constants. Joyce Cary's novels cannot be attenuated as life alone in the free will of the individual as done by Andrew Wright or the shaping of a private world giving the impression of an indeterminate universe as expounded by Robert Bloom or the individual and society as worked out by Golden Larsen. The perspective in Joyce Cary, from his criticism and the novels, is Reality as the subsequent chapters will expound and illustrate.

CHAPTER II

Primitive Reality

Joyce Cary (1888-1957) is a fascinating and mature novelist. His life, to write of it briefly, was chequered and one of hardship, physical distress and an exacting search for scholarship and a writer's calling. He belonged to an Anglo-Irish family of Devonshire. Born in North Ireland, he came over to England and visited Ireland later in life. He studied at school at Tunbridge Wells and, later, at Clifton College. He stated life as a painter, first at Paris and later, at the Art school at the University of Edinburgh. He next went to Trinity College, Oxford. He joined the army and fought in the Balkan Wars 1912-1913. He, then, became a member of Sir Horace Plunkett's Co-operative Society in Ireland and eventually joined the Nigerian Political Service. He worked in Africa as Political Officer, joined the Cameroons Campaign 1915-1916 and was wounded at Mora Mountain. He was District Officer in Borgu, the only white man, and saw native life at first hand. He was invalided and forced to retire in 1920. The same year he settled in Oxford. From 1920 to 1932 during which he read a lot, Cary wrote and published nothing. In the second World War, Cary served on civil defence. In 1943 he once again visited East Africa as political adviser. In 1946 he had a chance to visit India for a few months. He retured to Oxford where he led a sequestered life of study, struggle and toil to become a novelist. He was fatally struck by muscular atrophy and died on March 29, 1957.

He wrote fifteen novels, thirteen published in the Carfax Edition and two published by Michael Joseph, London. His sixteenth unrevised novel was edited by Winifred Davin and posthumously published in the Carfax Edition in 1959. He wrote four novels on Africa : *Aissa Saved* (1932), *An American Visitor* (1933), *The African Witch* (1936) and *Mister Johnson* (1939). These form a composite whole. They deal with real native life and his imaginative understanding of the same. His interest in native life was not like that of a historian making a record or that of an anthropologist from a scientific point of view. The artist in him cuts deep through the encrustrations of facts and life to get at the heart of Truth.

The African novels present Reality in the primitive world. Tribal races live at the instinctive level full of dark passions, suspicion, hatred and superstition. They live at the pre-conscious level ; they live not as independent individuals but within class and groups. Even within that limited social structure they are hemmed in by tribal rule and laws. They have their own gods and ritual and their own forms or worship. If an individual moves away from this tradition, he finds himself in an alien culture, no matter how civilized or Western that culture may be. He soon meets with disillusion and disaster and returns to his tribe and its old passions and practices or faces death. It is always the tribe or the group that wins.

Attempts are made by the whitemen to life the darkness from the lives of these tribals. The onslaughts on their primitive consciousness come, first of all, from missionaries who wish to bring the light of Christianity into the nocturnal shades of demonology which engulf the natives. The African novels of Cary deal with tribal patterns, the pagan world set off against Christian civilization. Cary looks at both with cool intellectual detachment and tries to see if the two can ever be at peace. The problem remains. The native has to undergo ample training before he can grasp the complexity of the new civilization. The pagans are not intellectually and psychologically equipped for a sophisticated outlook. It is this fact which gives rise to the dramatic conflict between the old and the new. The African world is in chaos because the christian values are too complicated to fit into the pagan society. Cary analyses the problem of religion and its implications which fall flat on the natives who have to accept a system that lies deep in their civilisation for hundreds of years.

> I think, from experience, that some Christian missions do not realize the effect of telling African primitives that God is 'Almighty' or 'Omnipotent' and allowing them, uncorrected, to suppose that this means not 'the final power in the universe' but the 'one who can do all things.' So that they blame God for a sore throat, and thank him for a fine day or a good bargain.
>
> I know that, in this respect, the Church is in the difficulty of all ancient institutions. It has inherited, like Parliament, articles of faith which were once taken in a literal sense but are now, by old believers, accepted as metaphors or symbols. And it can't change the form of expression without offending simple people.
>
> But the trouble is that converts are obliged to accept the letter. They start, so to speak, several hundred years behind the old believers, in an age of absolutism and intolerance. There is quite a large danger that the religious wars of the fifteenth and sixteenth centuries in Europe should be imported to Africa. There was such a war in Uganda in the eighties of last century.[1]

The first African novel is *Aissa Saved*, published in 1932, after three years of gestation. It poses the problem at the group level. The setting is Nigeria. There are two sets of characters which subdivide into other groups. On the one hand we have the Africans classifying into the natives and the christianised pagans. On the other hand, there are European characters represented by the Carrs at the religious level and Bradgate at the official level. The Carrs and Bradgate are not on good terms. The Carrs deeply resent any interference by Bradgate in their religious affairs, while Bradgate, a religious agnostic, feels an official responsibility to check the proselytization tac-

1. Joyce Cary, Prefatory Essay to *Aissa Saved*, Carfax Edition (Lodon, Reprinted 1960), pp. 8-9.

tics of the Carrs. The perpetual clash between the two African groups reveals a big psychological gap between the Europeans and the Africans.

The pagans have been taught to denounce and scoff at their own pagan cult without understanding why they feel superior to be christians. The pagans, who have not gone deep into the true meaning of Christianity, fight among themselves for reasons that are ridiculous. The pagans do not accept any explanation for the drought and bad prices. The judge explains to them that the slump is the result of the war and the bad crops due to the weather. To the Pagan chief, "this white man does not know anything about our country and the Emir is tired and does not care about anything. These rulers want to keep us quiet, to sound us to sleep. But we shall not be sent to sleep. We shall look for this person who has cursed our crops and stopped the rain : until we die we shall look, for we are not Mahoadans or Christians who lie down in trouble like a dog waiting to be whipped'. (p. 30). The primitive mind, not trained to think on scientific lines and not amenable to logic and common sense, attributes the sudden calamities to the supernatural agency that has to be propitiated. Superstitions govern sheir daily existence. The primitive mind is affected by exciting scenes and ritualistic performances. The primitives, because their thinking is not mature, get emotionally worked up and yield to the thrill of the moment. Ecstasy and common reaction is typical of the primitives. Cary describes the tribal instincts and gestures and the orgiastic dance, capturing its maddening and frenzied modulations in an extraordinary prose pattern :

> Some while walking clapped their hands and sketched the movements of the ritual dance, jerking their hips, bending their knees, many of the younger men and women to eager and excited to wait for the drums, were dancing fiercely, leaping, squatting ; the sweat ran down their backs, they were already in a trance, their eyes fixed, their muscles jigging like parts of a machine. They threw off their loin cloths and did not even hear the yells of

> encouragement from the crowd, who themselves carried away by the sight of them began also to leap, whirl, utter shrill cries which sounded like a defiance and an appeal. Not only the debtors, beggars, prostitutes, lepers, diseased wretches, ruptured children, syphilitic girls, idiots and outcasts, but those who seemed strong and well and to have no cares, leapt and grimaced with fierce, greedy cries and wild gestures which seemed to throw off heavy burdens of fear and anxiety : which said : 'I don't care for anybody, I don't care for anything. I'll do what I like this time.' (p. 54)

But characters in the novel live apart from each other. The Carrs are religious dogmatics, although they intend to deliver the natives from their state of ignorance and render a splendid service by setting up a hospital. Equally helpful is bradgate who thinks that the bridge he going to construct will bring the place a lot of good. It is the failure of the Europeans to communicate on the emotional plane that is responsible for the unresponsive attitude of the natives. Bradgate rationalizes instead of seeking emotional identification with the natives' .fficulty arising from the drought. He lectures rationally to the natives on the food shortage at Berua. The people ignore this connect the drought with the tribal curse : they had no alternative left but to sell their children :

> There has never been a whole year's drought in Yanrin because it is too near the sea. Moreover, I set for food to Berua, and next week I am going to fetch it. If the merchants here put up their prices. I shall sell this at a low price. No one will be allowed to starve. Above all, you must not sell your children. I am told that some children have disappeared from Kolu. It's a very bad thing. It is against the law to sell children on any account whatever.
>
> The people listened with blank faces, expressing nothing. They knew that it was not at all sure that rain would fall. History informed them that Yanrin had once been cursed by Oke so that not rain but burning cinders fell upon the land for ten years. They were con-

vinced also that it was better to sell children at the beginning of a famine when they were strong and able to walk, than later when they were already unfit to travel ; better then than to let them die. As for the unlawfulness, they knew there was no danger of punishment. For adoptions were lawful, and it was not possible to distinguish between adoption by persons desiring a child to love and cherish from one by those intending to make it a drudge or barter it to a husband or a brother. The one couple often became the other after a few years. (pp. 116-7)

They try to sift Bradgate's thought and do so most quaintly :

It seemed to them all that Bradgate was talking nonsense, but they listened patiently and respectfully and did not think badly of him because (they said) it is his business to tell these tales. They were only perplexed to know his object. But it was generally agreed that his objection to the selling of children, as also to slavery, was religious, because there was no reasonable explanation for it. (p. 11[illegible]

There is no broadening of the feeling of fellowship. The Carrs and Bradgate do not have an imaginative apprehension of the reality of native life. These Englishmen cannot see what Henry James comprehended :

Humanity is immense, and reality has a myriad forms...... Experience......... is an immense sensibility.[2]

The Pagan beautiful Nigerian women Aissa, later a christian convert, becomes the central figure in the novel. Aissa swings between her pagan instincts and Christian faith. Her personality shapes itself under recurring impulsive drives of fear and joy. But in an atmosphere where the mode of life of the natives is not favourable to the formation of individualized groups, Aissa enjoys the power of the imagination. When her imagi-

2. *Henry James : Collected Literary Criticism*, ed., Morris Shapira (London, 1963), p. 56.

nation is in abeyance, she is at one with the native crowd and breaks into hysteria :

> She leapt before Gajere three feet into the air, rocked before him on her haunches, beat herself against him and nearly threw him down ; she felt that she could dance better and jump higher than anyone had ever done before : she screeched obscenities which seemed to her so amazingly and unexpectedly witty that she laughed until she choked. (p. 55)

Seized with fear, Aissa has the foreboding of an evil spirit overpowering her. She has the sudden consciousness of having perpetrated a crime. Aissa, whenever she breaks away from the christians and joins the company of her people and her husband Gajere, is overjoyed. Although Aissa is without complex motives that constitute an individual personality, her imagination is more active and creative than that of the crowd of which she is also a member. Under the unconscious creative urge, Aissa is driven to the sacrifice of her child Abba, and self-mutilation in pursuance of the demand of both christians and pagans for rains. The same christians who save Aissa from the callous treatment of her village folk drag her away into the ants' nest.

Aissa, worn-out, drops into sleep. But in the morning she strives to pull herself away from the ant-heap. Cary describes in vivid language and metapher :

> She rolled on them, thrashed them with her forearms, crushing them by hundreds. But they were soldier ants born and bred for self-sacrifice. (p. 211)

The tempo of Cary's description rises in the last chapter for movement to movement to a gathering crescendo :

> Their bites like fire obliged her to call out, her shrieks were heard for along time by the Ketemfe people, but no one dared to go into the wood.

Her body is now weak and lacerated but her soul has a

prophetic vision. The vision itself is chimerical and fantastic—the christian God with pagan ties :

> Immediately the sky was rolled up like a door curtain and she saw before her the great hall of God with pillars of mud painted white and red. God, in a white riga and a new indigo turban, his hands heavy with thick silver rings, stood in the middle and beside him the spirit like a goat with white horns. Abba was sitting on its back looking frightened and almost ready to cry. One of the angels was holding him and putting his cap straight. The others were laughing at him and clapping their hands. (p. 211)

The climax in the last chapter brings out two characteristics of Joyce Cary the novelist. The first is the linguistic aspect of his art where words are so arranged as to give a vivid picture of events and persons involved. This is one of the achievements of the modern novel. A novel can be dramatic and provocative, but it can also be an instrument for subtleties of language and a whole range of effects. The prose texture of Cary in this last part of the novel is an example of the creative form, the well-shaped container for the theme. The second is the subject or Idea aspect of the novel. Cary writes that 'all great novelists have a theme, an idea of life profoundly felt and founded in some personal and compelling experience'.[3] He gives this in the finale where the distinction between objective reality and subjective experience is brought out. The novel presents a vague and confused idea of the dramatic existence of Aissa and her psyche. *Aissa Saved* illustrates powerfully the paradox of primitive reality, the theme in the novel.

In *An American Visitor* the colonial world is placed against the changing reality of primitive culture. This colonialism oscillates between materialism and idealism. Bewsher whose sole intention is to weave the Birri tribe into a fabric of unity is no doubt keen on arousing the sentiments of nationalism among them and Cary seems to sympathise with Bewsher, 'a

3. Joyce Cary, *Art and Reality* (New York, 1961), p. 174.

man who may have developed, like so many of the Nigerian pioneers, some odd notions, but who had nevertheless a consistent idea of what he was driving at, to preserve and develop the rich kind of local life which is the essence and the only justification of nationalism'. (p. 133). Bewsher testifies to his sense of idealism when he obstinately refuses to permit the commercial-minded Cottee and his company to set up tin mines and tries to adjust the African psychology to their own religio-mythical tradition :

> His real idea was that since the typical pagan worship was in itself a cult of life, and especially of this life, so that to pagans the life and passions of men extend through all being, animals, trees, even the sun and moon, the thunder god would be an excellent representative or saint of material energy, of all-pervading electrical force. As he said, Thunder is literally the sound or voice of that energy. (p. 132)

This passage gives us a vision of the antique world which anthropologists try to recreate. Much of that world and beliefs are based on hypotheses. Nature is invested with gods. These gods live and even die as Sir James George Frazer in that epoch-making book of anthropology *The Golden Bough* written massively in thirteen volumes states : 'Man in fact created gods in his own likeness and being himself mortal he naturally supposed his creatures to be in the same sad predicament'.[4] Cary perceives the principle of life of primitive man who projects his own life in the universe.

The missionary Dobson with his sense of christian ethics, finds pagan faith and religion unethical. He objects to Bewsher's sympathy for the Birri on the basis that the natives' 'peculiar religion had no ethics'. Bewsher's defence is described by Cary in the former's early approach to religion, which presents the basis for building up a higher doctrine. One should not destroy but build up :

4. Sir James George Frazer, *The Golden Bough* ; Part III, The Dying God (London, 1956), p. 3.

> For instance, they would make it a sin to impair or damage the fullness of being. In fact, by that device any kind of ethic, the christian if necessary, could be injected. 'Ethics are the simplest thing in the world. Everybody knows what's good, and you can shove it into any religion. But the trouble is to get a good religion, a good sort of form, to shove it into. You can't invent a religion. It's got to grow—and here we have old Ogun well rooted in and quite enjoying the climate'. (pp. 132-3)

In his extreme desire to keep his Birri safe from foreign contemination he never gives into the views of others and we see him in the role of a dictator, though slightly liberal, until the end :

> And with federation accomplished he could afford to let the traders in. In fact, he would want them, for he would need money to build the court houses and markets and to make the roads, and that would make his peace with the government. The missions were another pair of shoes. They got at the women, at the very foundations of the domestic system. Think of the Dobsons at Nok and Pare, thoroughly sincere, active, intelligent people with their whole minds on the job of winning souls, and all the knowledge and experience of civilization behind them. No Birri would have a chance against them. They'd play the devil in no time. That would be putting the pike into the pond and no mistake.
>
> He would bar the missions altogether. It would take five years at least, perhaps ten or twenty, to form a thoroughly useful native creed and ritual out of the *ju ju*, and pump in the right kind of ethicks. Play the game. (p. 220)

But it is central to the paradox of Cary that the Birri who are supposed to idolise Bewsher are up against him. Bewsher, under the impression that Birri is safe from turmoil, insists that the rioting pagans are striving for peace. Bewsher's commitment to the uplift of the natives' cultural conditions ironically leads to his death at the hands of the Birri.

Cottee is a foil to Bewsher. Always guided by commercial motives but intelligent, he is ever ready to capitalize on the confusing realities of the situation. Bewsher's imaginative participation in the hopes and fears of the natives is in sharp contrast to Cottee's ego-centric intelligence and the former's idealistic notions clash with the latter's purely materialistic outlook. Cottee is no doubt practical and of an accomodative temperament. The reader may agree with Cottee when, reacting to Bewsher's attempt to keep the Birri insulated against any change, he thinks, 'For even if civilization meant for the Birri a meaner, shallower kind of life, how could any man hope to fight against it when it came with the whole drive of the world behind it, bringing every kind of gaudy toy and easy satisfaction ? (p. 234). It will not, however, be correct to assume that Cary admires Cottee in spite of his lack of moral sense to exploit the weakening situation and denigrates Bewsher who clings to his faith so deggedly and which reduces him almost to a comic portrait.

Before Bewsher, Gore pales into insignificance. Smug in his Victorian comfortable existence Gore represents the authoritarian dogmatism and is hardly capable of planning a future for the Birri. His only regret is that the old world is dying out. The reason why Cottee is more intimate with Gore than with Bewsher is quite obvious. Gore thoroughly lacks in vision and faith in an idea. That is why he shows no objection to Cottee's mining prospects and tries to impose conventional rules on Bewsher. Whereas Bewsher, because of his sureness of purpose, an awareness of the problems facing the natives, is jibed at and disliked by Cottee.

Cary's introduction of Marie Hasluck, an American character, into the scene of British Colonialism in Africa service an artistic interest to give clearer perspective to his idea. Commenting an Cary's delineation of this character writes Warren G. Grench :

> He depicts not the man who knew coolidge, but the giri who read Thoreau ; and though Cary looks at the American with her head in the clouds rather than the American with his feet in the muck, he offers no more flattening picture than the celebrators of Hollywood burial rites. He leaves the reader with the notion that undisciplined idealism may be as destructive as self-seeking materialism if it rests upon the same inadequate philosophical foundation.[5]

It is interesting to note that Marie's peculiar idealism never takes concrete shape. At the beginning she is found instigating the Birri against the British officials for 'self-determination' and thereby trying to spread anarchy. She is drunk, as it were, with her hopes of a 'golden age' in Birri. As the story develops, she flirts with Gore and then comes under the charms of Bewsher. Cary's irony manifests itself when, as a housewife, Marie, so enamoured of the Birri, does not even hesitate to send for the police force to put down the rioters. The reader glances back and wonders what has happened to Marie's lofty idealism and her high conception of the noble Birri. Her idealism remains a fantasy and not an offshoot of the Creative Imagination. She is a unique example of a split personality who does not know what she is actually driving at. It is ridiculous to see a robust optimist like Marie relapse into pessimism :

> It was not until a sudden rush threw her against a wall and swept Obai completely away that she did for a moment expect to be killed, and then she did not feel frightened or angry so much as resigned. It wouldn't matter much. What turned up from the bottom of her mind was that very pessimism which always disgusted her. (p. 68)

At the conclusion of the novel, after Bewsher's death, that Marie Hasluck changes her concept of the noble Birri in the course of her bitter experiences which lead to self-discovery and a clearer insight into human nature.

5. Warren G. French, "Joyce Cary's American Romer Giri", *Texas Studies in Literature and Language*, II (Autumn 1960), p. 282.

Edward Wagen Khecht writes : 'Fiction is neither myth nor prophecy ; it is a thing grounded on patient observation of human nature'.[6] This is what Cary does in the novel. A sentimental idealist Marie Hasluck changes into a practical realist. She in freed from her delusion of a Golden age. She clings to her beliefs until she is pushed by circumstances into a self-realisation and becomes convinced of the truth of suffering and sacrifice under the impact of painful reality. What she fails to understand is that nobody, though she does naively apportion the blame to herself, is responsible for Bewsher's death. Warren G. French overlooks the main implications by summarily dismissing Marie's idealism as 'undisciplined'.[7]

Bewsher's death is inevitable. The following passage foreshadows Bewsher's impending and however selflessly he may have worked to improve the lot of the natives and encourage their nationalism :

> For though Bewsher himself had broken the old narrow tribalism of the Birri, it was Henry who made them eager for experiment. As for Obai, he went round the villages like a madaman preaching war against Bewsher and the whites. Let the truce last for ever, let the Birri join together in a great nation like the fulani and the Yorubas. Then they would be among the greatest nations in the world and all would fear them. The whites would fly before them. (p. 164)

The novel gives dramatic objectivity and gains in points of view, which is an important aspect of the novel. E.M. Forster writes :

> Indeed this power to expand and contract perception (of which the shifting view-point is a symptom), this right to intermittent knowledge—I find it one of the great advantages of the novel-form, and it has a parallel in our percep-

6. Edward Wagen Knecht, *Cavalcade of the English Novel* (New York, 1954), p. 45.

7. Warren G. French, *op. cit.*, p. 282.

tion of life. We are stupider at some times than others ; we can enter into people's minds occasionally but not always, because our own minds get tired ; and this intermittence lends in the long run variety and colour to the experiences we receive.[8]

The characters in *An American Visitor* analyse Bewsher's life, each from the point of view of his own character. Dobson is unchanged and emphasizes the place of God :

> The world without a provident and loving God has been compared with a lunatic asylum, but this is quite inadequate to describe the horror of the conception. Can we really imagine a world without justice, mercy, or indeed any object at all, a ceaseless warfare of face against race, in which it is equally possible for good men and bad to perish without the smallest advantage, in which we may say the good are more open to destruction than the bad just as in a quickly destroyed by the most violent and ruthless. In this war, moreover, not merely a whole race but its culture, the noblest accomplishment of a nation, could disappear like a stone into the sea without leaving a trace or even a recollection. (pp. 217-8)

Cottee looks at Bewsher's death from his usual loss and gain angle. He will not care to assess Bewsher's contributions, but sees that Marie, now a widow, is financially benefited by her husband's death :

> ...how unnecessary it was to produce and indulge all these mornful ideas. Monkey Bewsher had lived a good life and died the best kind of death, quick, unexpected, and in the midst of his prime. Marie no doubt was to be pitied. She had lost her Bewsher. But on the other hand she had inherited a pretty good income : she would be a well-off young widow instead of a wandering journalist of doubtful reputation and more doubtful future. She was placed in life on a sound financial basis. (pp. 233-4)

8. E M. Forster, *Aspects of the Novel*, Penguin Books (1963), p. 88.

But that Bewsher's death confuses the mind of even a cold, calculating exploiter like Cottee is borne out at the end when Marie, out of profound respect for Bewsher, kneels by his grave :

> That was the annoying thing. He would not mind kneeling himself if that was the proper procedure, but was it ? Gore met his eye in passing but without any change of his own features, which appeared even more melancholy, more hollow-eyed and hollow-checked than usual. Holding Marie's hand he bent towards her with that grand air which she herself had described when she said that Mr. Gore always made her think of king Arthur at the court of Mark Twain.
>
> Cottee, disappointed of sympathy in this quarter, reflected again that the man was a demned official and probably enjoyed ceremonies like this. There was a good deal of hokum about him too. (pp. 238-9).

Cary's philosophy is that in the very act of creation lies the seed of destruction. The creation moves through the lives of a group of foreigners—Bewsher, Gore, the Dobsons, Cottee, Marie Hasluck, the American, after whom the novel is named. They are shown in a variety of attitudes and action which criss-cross each other in a drama of conflicts. The romantic Marie Hasluck is disillusioned and the well meaning Bewsher is sacrificed. The truth lies in the irony of human life. The circumtances of Bewsher's death remind us of Frederick's thoughts of Catherine in Ernest Hemingway's *A Farewell to to Arms* :

> If people bring so much courage to this world the world has to kill them to break them, so of course it kills them.[9]

There is movement in the evolution of this idea in Cary's novel and no 'indeterminate stasis' 10 as Robert Bloom asserts.

---

9. Earnest Hemingway, *A Farewell to Arms*, Penguin Books (1955), p. 193.
10. Robert Bloom, *op. cit.*, p. 48.

The novel further does not deal, as Golden Larsen States, with British Colonialism.[11] There is a deeper strain in the novel. It focusses native reality as an area of darkness which swallows up the intruder.

The third novel, the 'most comprehensive African novel', is *The African Witch* (1936). It was written after initial hesitation because Cary wanted 'to avoid the African setting which, just because it is dramatic, demands a certain kind of story, a certain violence and coarseness of detail, almost a fabulous treatment to keep it in its place...'[12] Lest the theme of the novel be misunderstood. Cary himself had to clarify it : 'My book was meant to show certain men and their problems in the tragic background of a continent still little advanced from the Stone ge, and therefore exposed, like no other, to the impact of modern turmoil'.[13]

The novel poses a problem of recreating primitive life in the twilight of history. It takes us through nightmarish descriptions of primitive life steeped in witch craft, superstition, magic and the psychosis of fear. The natives of Rimi in Nigeria still live within a tribal pattern that dates back to more than a thousand years in human history. In 'the toilsome ascent' of man from savagery to civilization, magic precedes religion.[14] Later, the two mingle and religion is inseparable from magic as in *The African Witch.* The primitive religion of *ju-ju* is aptly described by Cary through one of the characters, Aladai, as 'the religion of the blood, the race, the old crocodile'. (p. 293). Elizabeth Aladai is the *ju-ju* priestess who dominates the novel, and casts a sinister spell over the unthinking masses. Cary explains the role played by a *ju-ju* priest in the native life :

---

11. Golden L. Larsen, *op. cit.*, p. 29.

12. Joyce Cary, Prefatory, Essay to *The African Witch*, Carfax Edition (London, Reprinted 1961), p. 11.

13. *Ibid.*, p. 12.

14. Sir James Frazer, *op. cit.*, p. xxv.

> In Africa, a *ju-ju* priest has a power of life and death which resides in him personally. He has knowledge and training : he has to be initiated, like priests elsewhere, but he must also have a quality which marks him off from others--the quality of power. Woman may have the quality as well as a man, and then she may become a priestess. The power is real, and so no one would dream of setting it aside by artificial rules limiting priest craft to one sex or caste. (p. 33)

The *ju ju* priestess Elizabeth possessed potent magical powers derived through the spirit of the *ju-ju*. She knew her people : 'She knew not only all the village gossip, but the characters of almost everyone connected with the victim and her family'. (p. 33). Her very appearance caused dread :

> As she approached the people, their faces, confident, lively a moment before, became rigid with terror. They knew that they were not witches, but the terror of the *ju-ju* woman's presence turned their bones to water. (p. 32)

Elizabeth famous for and skilled in identifying the witch responsible for the death of a child is a mystifying figure in her performance :

> Elizabeth had now no conscious will. She put from mind all the evidence that she had heard. She had placed herself under control of the *ju-ju* spirit, and now she felt spirit swelling and spreading through her whole body. She released her muscles—her arms hung like bags of lead on the aching hands of the girls—she softened her legs, bending them at the knees, making her flesh soft for the penetration of the spirit.
>
> She was not conscious of her direction. Yet the girls felt her turn them this way and that, by a slow pressure, as she glided through the rigid, breathless crowd.
>
> For half an hour she sought. Then, as she was passing close by the plaintiff's group, her hand jerked suddenly out, as if worked by a string, and gripped Osi by the wrist.

> She continued to hold the girl, who stood staring at her with an expression of foolish wonder. Her husband, father-in-law, the whole of her family, had already shrunk back from her. Osi's tongue appeared between her trembling lips ; she looked found and smiled, as if to say, 'This is silly.'
>
> Elizabeth, meanwhile, stood still in her trance. She shivered and uttered a deep sigh : her eyes opened slowly. She looked at Osi, and appeared as much surprised as the girl herself. (p. 34)

No women is a born witch. The people accuse Ibu of being a witch which she is not. Cary who is an omniscent novelist in the early novels comments on the tragic result of this false accusation by which intelligence is defeated by the forces of paralysed mind :

> Ibu, though stupid with terror, confusion of mind, misery, cold, and hunger, was an intelligent child. This quality had probably been her ruin. All intelligent, good-looking persons are exposed to jealousy, and jealousy is the subconscious source of the hatred with produces injuries—from injuries, fear ; and from fear, an accusation of witch-craft. In this way Africa has destroyed, every year for some millions of years, a large proportion of its more intelligent and handsome children. (p. 68)

The native has no individual existence. He is under the full away of heard instinct. The external stimuli stir the primordial urges to action and large numbers form a single crowd. Cary sees this aspect of native personality :

> They were simply nerve centres, intoxicated by noise, and the stimulation of various glands by hatred, fear, rage, and excitement, to make more noise and to produce more hatred and blood lust, not consciously directed at any special object. They would have murdered anybody at the slightest direction from outside. They only wanted cruelty, blood, more stimulation—the only way to release. (p. 214)

The kernel of truth is that the primitive mind in the grip of this uncanny *ju-ju* spirit comes in contact with the dark reality. This is the kind of art which a novelist must show for, as Henry James writes, 'you will not write a good novel unless you possess the sense of reality'.[15] (Of course Jame's reality, different from Cary's, is drawn from sophisticated society).

The novel next moves on to the problem of Races. The whites are once against the natives as we noted in *Aissa Saved.* The external polish decent manners of the wbites betray their hollowness when they look upon the natives as no better than brutes. The inacapacity of the whites for emotional identification with, and, a sympathetic understanding of, the natives create ugly situations. This gulf becomes apparent when at the very opening of the novel the native Aladai, educated in Oxford, crosses over into the racecourse of the whites and later embarrasses the entire while party by his presence at the Scotch Club. The duel between Rackham, a white, supposed to be free from colour complex and apparently sober, and Aladai gives a dramatic climax to racial antagonism. Aladai, no matter how completely he may have adopted what is best in the European civilization, is looked down upon as a member of an inferior race. The whites cannot tolerate the native culture and forget that the cultural character of a person is not determined by his physical characteristics. The whites and the natives are racially isolated and socially segregated. Aladai who tells Judy Coote, an intelligent white women, how freely he used to move in high circles in England is puzzled to find himself badly treated by the white minority before a large number of the natives who call him the 'prince' and are going to elect him the next Emir. The lack of mutual understanding causes the wide gulf which, according to Cary's analysis of the savage mind, 'it so great that the bush negro does not concern himself with it. His indifference to the white man and his ideas is founded on a feeling of difference so profound that his mind will not attempt to pass over the gap'. (pp. 148-9)

---

15. Henry James, "The Art of Fiction", *The House of Fiction,* ed., Leon Edel (London, 1962), p. 31.

There are, of course, some characters who try to rise above race complex and understand the other side with an open mind. Even the native through feeling, if not thought, can transcend the barrier. Such is the attitude of Akande Tom whose state of mind is described in a remarkable passage :

> When Akande Tom had put on over a naked skin linen coat, trousers, cloth cap, and black goggles, he felt as near a white man as it was possible for him to be, and en joyed in exaltation which might possibly be compared with that of risen soul on his first morning in paradise. Because, for Akande Tom, the change was not only one of appearance, but of being and power. (p.149)

While other white characters huddle together in their isolated circle, Dr. Schlemm, a missionary, moves out among the natives, leaving aside his intellectual snobbery. Both are self-effacing and because they aim at a higher purpose they are bound to be knocked out. Dr. Schlemm is betrayed by his disciples and Akande Tom, desirous of civilizing himself, is entrapped by the *ju-ju* tricks of his wife, Elizabeth.

Cary presents the whites as outwardly well-mannered but emotionally immature. On the slightest provocation they ignore the decency and decorum so essential to club life and resort to violence. Cary's irony hints at the uncivilized instincts or impulses of these civilized beings. Rackham's fight with Aladai simply because Dryas Honeywood, a charming white lady, spent the night with the blackman alone in the forest, illustrates the point. Equally ironical is the change in the character of Aladai. At first, a sensible energetic young man, intoxicated with European civilization and disgusted with his own Rimi civilization which is crippled by superstitious practices, Aladai impresses and convinces Judy Coote, the English girl, of his passionate desire to elevate his country to a civilized level through education, criticises the *ju-ju* practice as outdated, and wins the reader's sympathy by his efforts to be friendly with Dryas Honeywood inspite of the latter's scornful attitude towards him. Against the background of the *ju-ju* practices which control the primitive mind, Aladai's insistence on education raises an important issue. The reader is shocked by his lack of mental poise when, after his confrontation with Rackham, he develops bitterness and animosity against the whites. Aladai, the civilized African, sinks into his primitive self. He hates his European dress and incites the natives : 'War has come to us. It can't be avoided, except by cowards'. (p. 210). There is a tragic collapse from his sublime conception of universal art to his belief that only war with the white race is the solution to the problem.

The *ju-ju* hater comes under the spell of his sister Elizabeth, the *ju-ju* priestess, and is helpless before her. Though he once scientifically explained that '*ju-ju* was a false thing—a fear in the mind ; a fear put into the mind to make people suffer' (p. 290) he now sees that this weird power permeates the entire atomosphere and still remains a big mystery to him :

> It does not seem natural. Nature wants to live—not to die. Why should the best blood want to pour itself out ? Why does the blood love pain as well as joy ? What is this spite and jealousy in flesh ? Why do people cut themselves for the *ju-ju* ? What is the god of nature—this reasoning of blood soaked for a million years in the agony of beasts ? (p. 292)

Like other central figures, Aladai, whose imagination roves over a wide field and who can identify himself with the sufferings and miseries of his people and feels impelled to ameliorate the living conditions of the Rimi does not triumph and dies. He is educated, but must end up as a savage, thirsty for blood and violence.

The African world is so confused in *The African Witch* that it is doubtful whether education, which is the only remedy for backwardness put forward by the novel's hero, Aladai, is conducive to cultural awakening and growth. In this context it is quite pertinent to know Cary's own view on the issue and in consideration of the existing reality, he does not seem to agree that education 'would abolish barbarity and violence. The contrary is true. Education would bring in more violence, more barbarities ; it would break up what is left of tribal order, and open the whole country to the agitator'.[16] Cary, however, avers that 'the reason why Africa should be educated is that it is the duty, the religious duty, if you like, for all of us to desire enlightenment for all men, for all God's souls'.[17] He thus polarizes the two attitudes of the whites to the African problem of the natives.

Mister Johnson (1939) is the fourth African novel in which primitive reality continues, unchanged over centuries, inspite of the growing impact of English civilization. The setting of the story is Fada, a village town in Nigeria. The description of Fada gathers up the strands of its present and its past life :

> Fada is the ordinary native town of the Western Sudan. It has no beauty, convenience or health. It is a dwelling-place at one stage from the rabbit warren or the badger burrow ; and not so cleanly kept as the latter. It is a pioneer settlement five or six hundren years old, built on its own rubbish heaps, without charm even of antiquity. Its squalor and its stinks are all new....Poverty and ignorance, the absolute government of jealous savages, conservative as only the savage can be, have kept it at the first frontier of civilization. Its people would not know the change if time jumped back fifty thousand years. They live like mice or rats in a palace floor ; all the magnificence and variety of the arts, the ideas, the learning and the battles of civilization go on over their heads and they do not even imagine them. (p. 99)

The African Johnson, a youth of seventeen, after whom the novel is titled, in his obsession with a civilized way of life marries Bamu, a bush girl, and in his desire to make her a civilized lady, brings a set of the white lady's dress in high spirits. But to his utter disappointment, Bamu is indifferent to

16. Joyce Cary, The Prefatory Essay to *The African Witch*, Carfax Edition (London, Reprinted 1961), pp. 12-3.

17. *Ibid.*, p. 13.

him, but listens to her friend Falla who relates about the demon :

> But Niji—had twins—of course—some demon—had crept up—in her belly—when she was asleep—on the farm—but she knew—the people would drive her—so she did—one child for bush—behind yam store—she used to say—I fetch yam—she creeps out—suckles baby.
>
> Johnson gives a groan as Sozy kneads his feet. 'You damu women, always telling stories—I think you've got nothing else in your heads but all that nonsense about witches and devils and spells and corpse washers and twins'.
>
> He hears from outside : 'So the husband—was sick—he began to die—he goes to *ju-ju* man—*ju-ju* man says—bad devil in your house—he comes to find devil—he finds the baby—is the devil—a very bad devil—they all run out-set fire to house—but Niji comes back—gives a scream—runs into house—she's all burnt up—'. (pp. 108-9)

The natives enmeshed in cultural stagnation know nothing about progress and civilization. The commercial benefits that might accrue from the construction of a road linking the bush town to the outside world cannot kindle and enliven their blunted imagination.

Johnson's false pretension to his civilised status makes him appear ridiculous. He tries to emancipate himself from the tribal inhibitions, but he is too primitive to grasp the subtle and complicated processes of civilized life. He lives in an atmosphere where the possibility of developing individual contacts and widening the mental horizon is conspicuously bleak. His wife Bamu, far from coming out of the family circle, is ringed in within its harshness. She is insensitive to Sozy, an old woman, who stays with her, Cary gives a picture of Johnson's household which is a narrow world :

> Bamu listens in silence and then suddenly utters a scream like a parrot. "Sozy, the pepper". Old Sozy rushes out from behind the waterpot and rummages in the kitchen. Bamu goes

to find the pepper. Bamu never looks at Sozy, and never converses with her. Since Sozy belongs to another village and is, besides, old and rather stupid, she feels her to be a different species from herself. Probably she would react in the same way to a strange dog. She is kind to her, politely bears with her scatterbrains, and feeds her, but she does not give her a bed or a blanket. Sozy still lies all night trembling with cold, aching with rheumatism, in the narrow space between the water-pot and the well, but this is only because it has not occurred to anybody that she may be suffering. (p. 86)

Cary knows that the primitive society is not wholly an image of purity and innocence. Bamu, who is for the most part under the domination of her brother in her relations with Johnson, is not scheming and ill-intentioned even when she leaves her husband. Contrasted with Bamu is Waziri, a native corrupt official, who gets hold of confidential reports by bribing the none-too-clever clerks like Johnson. In the Waziri's acts can be seen the paralysed creative abilities of the native unable to think beyond the immediate material needs. The scene is between Waziri and Jonson, the one trying to persuade the other to hand over the King's letters for money :

> You want me to show you all the government letters, Waziri ?'
>
> Waziri laughs gaily and rocks ; Saleh looks still more supercilious.
>
> Johnson, for a greater effect, speaks in English, 'You say to me, Mister Johnson, you government man, you belong for de King, you know de King's thoughts, you lell me dem King's thoughts, I give you plenty money'.
>
> Waziri throws out his hands and cries in House. 'It is the custom, Mr. Bauli—'.
>
> Johnson jumps up with an indignant gesture. Benjamin, Ajali and the half-dozen boys from the station gaze upwards with intense interest. The whites of their eyes beneath the

iris are like thin crescent moons lying on their backs. They hold their breaths with excitement.

Johnson throws out his arm and raises his chin.

'I not Mister Bauli, Waziri, I Johnson—I belong for government. I belong for de King. I Mister Rudbeck's frien'—I no take money for King's letters, I no fit to such a ting'.

Waziri gets up and bows low. Saleh closes his eyes, as if overcome by the oppressive vulgarity of the scene.

'I surprised at you, Waziri'.

Waziri smiles, bows again, and rises with a perfectly blank, bored face, His eyes are also half closed, and his expression is that of the slum visitor who having finished the day's visits and smiled through a hundred smells, is suddenly projected into a still more revolting smell, which is actually outside her district.

'I think you forget I government man'.

Waziri answers in a flat voice, 'Pardon, I was told you were like the others, like Mr. Bauli, who was a very sensible man. Good night, Mr. Johnson, God prolong you'. (pp. 34-5)

Cary goes to the root of the disease that infects both worlds —the primitive and the civilized. The British Colonial government suffers from administrative lapses and is a mere shadow of its past glory, incapable of bringing any imaginative freshness to the problem impending the native progress. Rudbeck, the Assistant District Officer, and Bulteel, the Senior Officer, converse on the native civilization with incertitude as to what should happen to the tribal pattern of life :

'We're obviously breaking up the old native tribal organization or it's breaking by itself. The people are bored with it'.

'Yes, yes, and I'm not surprised', Bulteel says.

Rudbeck is greatly surprised. 'Don't you believe in the native civilization' ?

'Well, how would you like it yourself' ? Bulteel smiles at him sideways with a kind of twinkle.

'Then you think it will go to pieces' ?

'Yes, I think so, if it hasn't gone already'.

'But what's going to happen then ? Are we going to give them any new civilization, or simply let them slide downhill' ?

'No idea', Bulteel says cheerfully. (p. 167)

Budbeck understands that the natives in themselves are full of goodwill and good sense ; they can form an organization, but they are an 'obstructive mass blocking all creative energy, not from any conspiracy or jealousy, but simply from the nature of official rules and routine'. Bulteel, expedient, has no long-distance view of changes in native life and 'hopes that Rudbeck will soon get tired of malice and settle down, like the others, to do his job, as a job, fill in his forms, draw pay, play golf and bridge, bring up his family and instruct his own juniors in their turn, 'No long views—the age for long views ended twenty years ago—and above all, not too much zeal'. (p. 209)

The trouble with the civilized christian in this novel, too, is the same incapacity for sympathetic understanding and emotional involvement. This is the reason why Blore, conscious of British manners, 'really hates Johnson. The shouts and songs from the clerk's compound, during several nights, have filled him with what he takes for indigestion, but which is chiefly fear. All exuberance alarms him, as if he feels in it, from Nature itself, some threat to established things'. (p. 24). The British Officials are tied to their mechanical office-work and the pagan, with a mind closed to all frontiers of the changing world, takes excessive delight in acts of sensual gratification and physical restlessness.

On both sides progress is stagnant. Johnson is a hopeful case towards improvement. But he is, as it were, jolted out of his dream into squalied life by Gollup, an English ex-soldier, who, heavily drunk, loses his sanity and mercilessly beats his wife, Matumbi, in the same barbarous fashion as the natives. Cary created two types of characters representing two aspects of the reality of existence. Johnson moves from primitivism to civilization and Gollup falls from civilization to primitivism. Cary attempts to give a human dimension to the schizophrenic character of Gollup by reconciling the civilized and the brute in him :

> He has the air of one who has just defeated a dangerous enemy. In fact, Gollup always seems like an old solider on campaign in enemy country ; watchful, suspicious, enterprising, always on the alert always in fighting trim ; not too punctilious, scornful of convention ; but, for all his good nature, ferocious and ready at any moment for any kind of violence. (p. 131-2)

There is an ironic tone in the conversation between Celia and Rudbeck who seems to avoid any further query about the erection of the mat wall for the bathing pool which separates the whites from the black and which symbolizes the cultural barrier between the two races :

> Celia languidly swims ashore, and stands in her red trunks skimming her flanks and gazing at the mat wall. Johnson and the small boy hasten to throw a bath towel and a bathing gown over her. She says to Rudbeck, 'Why the wall, Harry' ?
>
> Rudbeck is in his shirt. He pulls on a pair of soldier's shorts and draws the tape at the waist. 'Peeping Toms'.
>
> 'But it's public road'.
>
> 'Much too public. Don't go away, Audu. (p. 152)

The conversation drifts on :

'Would you mind at Bournemouth or Brighton' ? Celia asks in an amused tone.

Rudbeck says nothing. He thinks he has made a fool of himself, but he can't be sure. He wishes he were sure, and he feels a vague resentment, as if somebody ought to have told him what to think.

'You're not jealous, are you ?'

'Good God, no—of a lotta apes like that'.

'But if they were really monkeys ?'

'Damn it all, Celia, why not let it go at that ? Or must you analyse everything I do ?' (pp. 152-3)

Rudbeck and Johnson in spite of their closeness are apart. The meeting of the two hearts seems a remote possibility, because they come from different cultural backgrounds. It is true that there is a sudden thrust of exhilaration in both Rudbeck and Johnson. Johnson's creative imagination finds free play during the period of his close association with Dudbeck. The latter's idea of road-building takes shape under Johnson's impetus. The task, when it begins, sends Johnson into a frenzy and he galvanizes the horde of workers in vigorous action. But after the road is completed, there is an absence of spiritual affinity between the two. Rudbeck charges Johnson with collecting road tax illegally and dismisses him from service and ultimately to his tragic death. It is this lurid streak in native darkness which accounts for the movement of the novel from an act of creation which having reached its climax culminates in the we-aring off of its importance.

One important feature that distinguishes *Mister Johnson* at once from the preceding novels is its concentration on the central protagonist who contributes to develop the plot—which, Edwin Muir calls 'the chain of events in a story and the principle which knits is together, to 18—' its logical climax.

18. Edwin Muir, *The structure of the Novel* (London, 1960), p. 16.

After having cursorily read the story which tells how Johnson, in his eagerness to become civilized, steals, embezzles, murders and is finally shot dead, one is apt to judge the novel as didactic but Cary himself does not want critical judgment.

> The restless movement irritates many readers with the same feeling, that events are rushing them along before they have time to examine them, to judge them, and to find their own place among them. But as Johnson does not judge, so I did not want the reader to judge. And as Johnson swims gaily on the surface of life, so I wanted the reader to swim, as all of us swim, with more or less courage and skill, for our lives.[19]

On closer analysis we know that Johnson's tragedy has deeper implications than meets the eye. Mr. Johnson evokes what may be called the emotional empathy of the reader. In *Aissa Saved* the reader fails to feel the reality of the heroine's experience. Johnson is an individualized portrait 'capable of surprising us in a convincing way'.[20] The critics agree on this point. Andrew Wright calls Johnson as 'one of the most fully realized characters in the entire canon'.[21] To Arnold Kettle Johnson is 'deeply pathetic in his complete vulnerability, enormously sympathetic and amusing in his superb vitality and courage'.[22] Enid Starkie makes a similar comment : 'Into the character of Mister Johnson himself he (Cary) has breathed life with loving sympathy'.[23] That other characters look at him differently testifies to his being a full-blooded individual character in his own right. Blore detests him, Celia is simply amused by him and calls him a 'Wog', Rudbeck puts him,

---

19. Joyce Cary, Prefatory Essay to *Mister Johnson*, Carfax Edition (London, Reprinted 1961), p. 10.
20. E.M. Forster, *op. cit.*, p. 85.
21. Andrew Wright, *op. cit.*, p. 61.
22. Arnold Kettle, *An Introduction to the English Novel*, II, Grey Arrow Edition (1962), p. 188.
23. Enid Starkie, "Joyce Cary : A Portrait', *Essays by Divers Hands*, ed., Joanna Richardson (London, 1963) New Series, XXXII, p. 128.

although formally, on the same human level. A round character passes through a series of situations and becomes wise through experience. Johnson, too, realizes his folly in prison which is also to be the place of his end.

Cary does not romanticise Johnson's fate. We know that Johnson retains all through his career his innocence and appears, even after the murder, a pure being. He is a keen aspirant to the white man's way of life, but his acquisition of English culture is superficial. He is deemed through his failure to understand an alien culture. Cary's own unequivocal comment lends sufficient countenance :

> I meant to create characters and leave them to act ; characters conceived with those springs of action which seemed to me most important in all character, working out their fates in a world charged throughout with freedom and individuality.[24]

In *Aissa Saved*, *An American Visitor* and *The African Witch*, there is looseness of structure which accounts for Cary's attempt to intellectualize the theme of 'Dark' reality. This reality has been more dramatically rendered in *Mister Johnson.* Cary in this novel pays particular attention to internal relationships of character and event. He has confined himself to producing and intensification of action, which is set going by the changing tension in the character of Johnson himself.

Cary wants the reader to be actively caught in the stream of events. He uses the present tense and discards that of the past tense. He explains this in a brilliant passage in the Preface :

> So if they are in the past tense he is in the past, he takes part in events that have happened, in history, over there. This is a true taking-part, whether the history is actual history or a novel. A reader can tremble still at the

24. Joyce Cary, Prefatory Essay to *Castle Corner,* Carfax Edition (London, Reprinted 1960), p. 6.

> crisis of Waterloo ; or rage at the fate of Huss. He has in War and Peace a concentrated and lasting experience. But it is still a special, an historical experience ; it derives much of its quality from the recognition of general causes, it is charged with reflection (such as a man among actual events may use even at a crisis, and in the middle of distress, but first withdrawing himself from among them), with comparison and judgment.
>
> But with a story in the present tense, when he too is in the present, he is carried unreflecting on the stream of events ; his mood is not contemplative but agitated.[25]

The African novels give us a glimpse into the reality of primitive life. The African natives, cut off from the external world outside the narrow circle of their superstitious beliefs and age-old tribal customs, find it difficult to communicate with the Englishmen on the logical plane. Their springs of action are primordial urges. The Englishmen, on the other hand, fail to understand the reality as it exists and even though they are well-intentioned, they make themselves appear ridiculous in the eyes of the natives. Civilized consciousness of a few characters, though a healthy symptom, is set at nought by native reality. The native's illusion that he is civilized before he has undergone rigorous training is ironical. The individual character who is above the general mass by virtue of his creative vitality has to work in a world that is hostile to him. In *Aissa Saved* objective reality and subjective experience are fused in creative language and metapher. In *An American Visitor* he gets to the dramatic or points of view. In *The African Witch* he succeeds in giving the novel of panorama or two cultures—primitive and modern. In *Mister Johnson* he gives communication through a living present in which the story moves.

---

25. Joyce Cary, Prefatory Essay to *Mister Johnson*, Carfax Edition (London, Reprinted 1961), p. 9.

CHAPTER III

Imaginative Reality

The two novels of childhood, *Charley is My Darling* (1940) and *A House of Children* (1941), take us on to a new segment of reality. Cary has a significant passage on the imagination :

> ... the imagination is always looking for significance ; both in the physical and moral world, that is its job, to put together coherent wholes, a situation with meaning, a place where the child does know, all the time, where he is.[1]

Here we have the complex of the Imaginative faculty at work : the capacity to select and to give meaning, to integrate the different fragments into an organic whole. With these basics Cary considers childhood in *Charley is My Darling*. He writes :

> The child is a born creator. He has to be, for though in sympathy he is one with those he loves, in mind he is alone. He has to do his own learning and thinking. And Nature, for his very necessary good, sets him to enjoy it. Any one can see how children enjoy discovery and reflection. But also how soon they are bored with what is known. It is as if Nature says to them, Go on, go on, there's plenty more that you must know' ; and has made the joy of discovery evanescent ; the imagination, like the appetite, perpetually greedy.[2]

1. Joyce Cary, Prefatory Essay to *Charley is My Darling*, Carfax Edition (London, Reprinted 1961), pp. 9-10.

2. *Ibid.*, p. 8.

The child imagination is like the Creative Imagination which Charles Morgan considers as essentially 'ecstatic not intellectual'.[3] The child's attraction for love becomes an act of his life, even as are his repulsions for the unsympathetic adult. The 'powerful imagination' of the child lacks judgment with its obvious dangers and Cary sees this :

> The suddenness of temptation or rather, inspiration which (like many that come to an artist) is so quick that he doesn't even notice it, it leaves no moment for reflection. The imagination sees its opportunity, its prey, and instantly leaps upon it.[4]

Cary next deals with juvenile delinquency which he would have us believe is not an inherent defect in the child's mental make-up but is due to want of guidance by parents and teachers. Cary writes :

> Children don't know where they are, and they do all kinds of evil (because it is just this sphere of good and evil that is puzzling them) to find out. A child will torture a cat or some other smaller child, in order to see what will happen, both to himself and the victim, and what he feels like in the new circumstances. The 'crime' is a moral experiment.[5]

The child, though confused, has his own imaginative reality.

Charley is My Darling (1940) presents Charley Brown, an adolescent of fifteen. He is an evacuee, one of a group of children born to the country, Burlswood, from London in the second world war. Charley's emotional ties with his parents are not well-knit. He faces a problem of adjustment. He is

---

3. Charles Morgan, "Creative Imagination", *English Critical Essay—Twentieth Century* (London, 1958), p. 64.

4. Joyce Cary, Prefatory Essay to *Charley is My Darling*, Carfax Edition (London, Reprinted 1961), p. 7.

5. *Ibid.*, p. 9.

under the supervision of the billeting officer, Miss Lina Allchin and her lieutenant, Phyllis Hawes. They try to be affectionate towards him and Charley values this : 'He is full of that gratitude with which a child, and especially a boy of his sensitive age, fifteen, responds to a sympathy'. (p. 12) Charley is emotionally unstable and is not satisfied with the new change. He resents discipline and refuses to submit to normal restrictions such as Miss Allchin is particular that the boy should not keep bad company. In the new set-up, he feels 'a kind of confusion which is like a splitting up of the brain into senseless fragments, and in that confusion he does or says things which astonish him and shame him for a long time afterwards. (p. 43). His imagination finds an outlet through drawing by which he is able to give expression to his creative urges and inner tensions. His drawing of the bull is an example : 'He puts in a blue cloud with red edges on the left and a red cloud with blue shadows on the right. The effect seems to him terrific : the bull now looks like a bull of blue fire with transparent horns full of flame. He gazes for another five minutes, enchanted by his own bull, and then puts in a third cloud and darkens the other two.' (p. 49). This is Charley's song of experience, his equivalent to Blake's 'Tiger, tiger burning bright'.

Miss Allchin becomes an obstacle as Charley consider her a threat to his self-realisation and tries to run away from her. He wants to enjoy his powers in total freedom uncontaminated by the practical demands of life. The young adolescent has a desire to experience himself as a pure spirit and this desire finds its external computerpart in reality seen from a great distance. Charley tells his boy friends stories woven out of his imagination. The story is about a castel—'with pictures like at Windsor Castle and marble statues and golden pillars .. — and carpets like grass all with flowers in em, years, and great bowls full of roses and every hight they ad fountains playing with coloured lights'. (p.57)

The Psychology of Adolescence

Through his imagination the adolescent, like the younger child, can leap over the barriers of time and space.

> He can transcend the limits of his own powers and vastly extend his reach.[6]

Charley lives in a climate of anti-intellectualism. He starts going to school, but soon he loses interest in his studies. We are told he 'finds it difficult to keep his mind fixed on industrial revolution or even the chief rivers of England'. (p. 122). His mind wanders and he looks out of the window and gazes on Mrs. Allchin, the mother of his supervisor, laying a brick-bath in the garden. His imagination works on the layout of a new rock-garden 'with pegs and string, at the end of the lawn, near the wall'. (p.135). His imagination blossoms forth in a garden lay-out. In spite of Miss Small's scoldings, he conjures up a vision and 'invents a story in which he steals many more stones and completes the whole rock garden, cave and canyon. Mrs. Allchin, staggering from hersick bed, sees this work with amazement, is carried away by her feelings, expresses her gratitude and appreciation. "An the old lady gives a sort of gasp—or eyes is all shining—Its' a fair knock-out, see-and she says to me : 'Charley, thess the best rock garden I ever saw'—and she says : 'Thank you Charley'. Ere, ere, come off it. She couldn't say that, not my old lady wouldn't—she's a real shorter—". (p. 132). This day dreaming 'permits the imagination to play with ideas that are immediate satisfactions of desired goals or purposes ......'.[7] In an anxiety he cannot concentrate, he easily becomes depressed : 'He recoils from home, from bed, from accepting the day's end. He feels like a man whose life has been a failure, longing for escape and yet reluctant to die'. (p. 139). The look garden symbolizes Charley's hunger for and vision of a new pattern of life. But since he cannot lose sight of the world he lives in, there is a subtle tension between the joy of imagination and dissatisfaction with social situations :

> He is as silent and absorbed as a monk in contemplation of the visions produced by his own devotion ; yet, like

---

6. Dr. Arthur T. Jersild, *The Psychology of Adolescence* (New York, 1957), p. 112.

7. Lester D. Crow and Alice Crow, *Adolescent Development and Adjustment* (New York, 1956), p. 308.

a monk, he is secretly bored, and he knows it. His contemplative peace floats like a golden cloud a hill-top ; within it is grey mist and the hill is a dreary solitude. (p.126)

When the garden is destroyed it is a stunning blow to his enthusiasm and drives him into utter frustration :

> His tone is full of tender sympathy for the lost rock garden. He is feeling for a friend, put upon and neglected, but still a friend. (p. 139)

Charley suffers from a sort of paranoid schizophrenia. He has delusions of grandeur and his hunger for imagination is insatiable. Followed by his friends he breaks into a house where the drawing room excites his imagination. He imagines that he is playing host to a thousand guests, and welcoming his gangster boys as gentlemen he says, "Scuse my butler being out, this evening e's gorn to see a friend at the Green Man. The chairs is real gold and the table is Italian marble with gold legs,'. (p. 269). Charley, if debarred from his delinquent acts, is active in his imagination because 'an adolescent who is willing to compromise to free himself from a conflict situation discovers that any action he takes to relieve tension is better from him than passive acceptance of emotion-disturbing conditions'.[8]

Charley's incessant craze for imagination should not be construed as his tendency to get lost in the realm of fantasies only. This reflects his tacit revolt against the world outside dominated by the grown-ups with their narrow beliefs and rigid moralities. It is with uncanny precision, Cary keeps to adolescent psychology in this novel. Lester D. Crow and Alice Crow in their book *Adolescent Development and Adjustment* perceptively state what may well apply to Charley :

> With self awareness comes the struggle for self-realization. He begins to want to make his own decisions and to experience freedom of action.[9]

8. *Ibid.* pp. 304-5.
9. *Ibid.*, p. 6.

It is not true that Charley is pathologically hostile to the society of his elders. He is sufficiently aware of his moral position. When he sees the girl Lizzie caught in Harry's arms, he gets a sudden insight. Sexual motivation is replaced by a new interest in women. His attitude towards them becomes one of respect and human sympathy :

> Charley, for the last year, has been especially contemptuous of all sentiment. He is old enough, precocious from life and town experience, to be excited by girls, but the excitement is still divided into two different parts, sexual and romantic. The first expresses itself only in obscene words, jokes and drawings on walls or lavatories ; the second, which is still a total excitement of his whole body, causes him to feel the most tender kindness towards actual of girls or women of any age who do him kindness or even smile at him. He at once thinks such women beautiful and plans to confer extraordinary benefits upon them. (pp. 79-80)

Charley takes extreme delight in the creations of his emagination. It is only when his imagination visualizing a new order is crushed that he resorts to wildness and delinquency. In moments of illumination he is not happy with his nefarious activities :

> He had been oppressed from the very first enterprise, the Burls House climb, by the sense of futility. He enjoyed planning and forcing an entry into a house, but he had no taste for rummaging or looting. After each robbery he seemed to be exactly where he was before ; and though he never allowed himself to think "This can't go on for ever— sooner or later I'll be caught", he felt it continuously. It was a drag on all his enjoyment even of some extraordinary feat or climbing as at Twyport. (p. 244)

Cary shows the conflict between the child and the adult. The grown-ups' society is incomprehensible and even disgusting to Charley. Lina, on her part, is surprised at Charley's odd behaviour and makes a frank admission of it to her friend Wandle :

> "I don't feel I know anything about children—I'm really the last person for a job like this. And you can do such frightful harm by not knowing.
>
> "You couldn't know that this young rescal was a car-thief."
>
> "I might have got to know him better—but children are so elusive, and I don't like to impose myself on Charley—He's so delightfully independent". (p. 171)

In spite of her tactful efforts to keep Charley under control and curb his delinquent tendencies, the moment he sees the group of boys of his own age, he cannot resist what Richard A Cloward and Lloyd E. Ohlin describe, in their analysis of delinquency, 'the boisterous ganging tendency'.[10] He is motivated by the same anti-social instincts, commits theft and burglary in a breath-taking sequence and becomes a problem child of juvenile delinquency. The irony underlying the title is clearly perceived as Charley, the 'darling' of everybody becomes a constant source of threat to the order and tranquillity of the place.

Charley's sense of loneliness springs from his unconscious sexual drives which seek to find fulfilment in his intensely passionate relations with his girl-friend Lizzie. Miss Lina fails to understand Charley's psychological conditions and the news that Lizzie is expecting a child before marriage infuriates her. She has believed that Charley will conform to the existing moral pattern of the adult society. Her onslaught is piercing. The boy's departure from and breach of this convention brings him a severe scolding from her :

> "I can't understand it", Lina says but obviously she is sure that in this situation, at least, she can't be wrong. "I didn't think you were like that".

10. Richard A. Cloward and Lloyd E. Ohlin, *Delinquency and Opportunity, A Theory of Delinquent Gangs* (New York, 1960), p. 55.

"Like what ?" Charley thought. "What am I like ?".

"It's so cruel and mean—and you don't seem to care a bit".

Charley is struggling against the woman's mysterious purpose, which he feels to be dangerous. He feels as if she is trying to push him into a dark place from which he will never escape. He has no words to describe a sense of guilt, a conviction of sin, but he feels by nervous imagination what they are.

"Arn't you ashamed of yourself, Charley—not even a little ashamed ?"

A huge blackness rises upon Charley and he makes a desperate leap to escape from it. He exclaims : "But Liz didn't say nothing –". (pp. 323-4)

Cary in the conclusion of the Prefatory Essay wrote with insight :

> Knowledge, in short, the experience of the mind, is just as important to a child's happiness and 'goodness' as affection, adventure ; above all, the knowledge of his own moral position. And the last is often most difficult for him to come by, not because he could not grasp a complex situation ('this is a grand deep but a bad one'), but because grown-ups do not trust the power of his imagination to form a picture in more than one dimension.[11]

In anguished childhood more than in happy childhood there is always the point of the child's moral position. He is misunderstood, motives are assigned to him, he strives to come up to adult propriety, he repents may be, but there is always the deep sense of frustration and eventual revolt. All this gamut of moods is illustrated in this encounter of Lina and Charley :

11. Joyce Cary, Prefatory Essay to *Charley is My Darling*, Carfax Edition (London, Reprinted 1961), p. 10.

> "Yes, miss, I'm sorry—I been bad—to everybody". Charley repents violently between sobs.
>
> Lina, too, is tearful. She congratulates the boy on his repentance : "Now I do hope for you, Charley : and you know I will always be your friend".
>
> She goes away happy and leaves him remorseful, still more confused than before. He complains to himself : "But she wouldn't listen—it wasn't like that".
>
> His violent emotion, which was remorse, now becomes anger. "Why did she go on at me ? She didn't even listen. It wasn't like that".
>
> He is enraged with Lina, not only on his own account, but because he feels that Liz, too, poor Liz—and wot was wrong with it ?"
>
> But he feels also unsafe. For now he can't think of Lizzie and himself together, without hearing Lina's judgment and catching her contemptuous feeling. All his lovemaking with Lizzie, which an hour before had the beauty of its happiness, now suddenly takes ugly and squalid shapes.
>
> He is angry, ashamed, bitter, and, above all, confused. He says to himself, artuing when argument itself is an expression of doubt : "It isn't like that—she don't understand. Lizzie and me—". (p. 325)

The end of the novel is poignant. Charley is caught by the constable. An unrelieved gloom, dark and sinister descends upon the child :

> Charley turns like an automation ; Lizzie, the polite little girl ready to do the proper thing, gets up and comes forward. Suddenly her face twists and instantly both children break into loud gasping sobs. But they stand before each other stiffly, as if at a children's dance lesson. (p.342)

Charley is led to the police car, 'Charley, blind, deaf and senseless, not knowing what is happening to him, steps down into the glittering dark'. (p. 343). He enters the car : "They'll smother me" he says. Lizzie faints. The sergeant thinks that it is due to hunger and thinks of a sandwich for her. There could be no sharper irony and better moral than this.

The imaginative gift which Charley possesses lends an individual to touch his Character. Apart from the gang mentality and crimes, he reiteratively escapes into the world of his own steeped in strange thrilling experiences, glorious visions, exciting plans and daring exploits. From such a world to the sordid is a depressing reversal. All through, he finds himself in a situation which is not favourable to his growth or his creative prospects. Cary's child character has creative vitality and is full of new possibilities but suffers from a sense of loneliness, because there is no understanding between the grown-ups and the children. The world cf the child, therefore remains unconnected and alienated from the real world.

In the next novel, *A House of Children* (1941) Cary passes from the realistic to the romantic plane. As *Charley is My Darling* deals with the problem of evil and crime in childhood, *A House of Children* deals with the beauteous world of childhood its innocence, its poetry and its sensation of living. *A House of Children* is narrated by Evenlyn Corner who recalls his boyhood. In this imaginative reconstruction, Cary considers the function of the artist 'in the creation on rational wholes'.[12] The perspective in this novel is of childhood seen in retrospect with its actual experience and events dramatized.

The novel has an autobiographical basis. Cary recalls that the sensation of childhood remained with him 'for more than fifty years'.[13] He replies to the question whether the novel is autobiography by stating that the names, places, and people

12. Joyce Cary, Prefatory Essay to *A House of Children*, Carfax Edition London, Reprinted 1961), p. 7.

13. *Ibid.*, p. 6.

are disguised'.[14] Furthermore, he speaks of the two characters in the novel, Evelyn Corner, that is, Cary himself and Hary, his elder brother. He writes of this double creation :

> But I notice that this elder brother is also myself, and I suspect that I divided myself in this way because I realized by some instinct (it was certainly not by reason) that the two together as a single character would be too complex for the kind of book I needed to write ; a book full of that clarity, the large skies, and wide sea views, which belong to the vision of my childhood.[15]

Cary affirms that the child, although he lives in his own world of fantasies and sensory impressions, is sensitive to the reality around by intuition. Defining intuition and its importance to the child he writes : 'Intuition, the recognition of the objective real in its own quality, is, of course, an essential function. The smallest children must have power to know. And they explore the world of things and events, of characters, with intense curiosity and concentration'.[16] This response to the objective world arouses some sensations in the child, but he is not emotionally involved in it. He is not even conscious of his own existence as Cary writes in the novel : 'Small children are thought happy, but for most of the time they do not even live consciously, they exist ; they drift through sensations as a pantomime fairy passes through coloured veils and changing lights'. (p. 9). Paul Schilder, making a subtle distinction between sensation through perception and experience through direct participation writes :

> Perceptions are experiences, like that of seeing a forest, without a particular inner participation in which the structure of the world is our chief interest. In emotions we are

14. *Ibid.*, p. 7.
15. *Ibid.*, pp. 7-8.
16. Joyce Cary, *Art and Reality*, Anchor Edition (New York, 1961), p. 47.

> aware of a great participation of the self and th body, when directed towards a situation which we perceive...we mean sensation when we consider a perceptual experience more in relation to what is happening in our body than to events in the outside situation ; and when we emphasize the relation between the perception in the outward world and the experience in our body.[17]

Nevertheless, the child's sensation arising from something unseen and unknown is beyond rational analysis. This is exemplified in the experience of two child characters, Harry the elder brother and Evelyn, the younger one :

> We shrieked together in joyful terror. We were growing drunk with expectation, which was increasing all the time. For in us children it was a pure passion and never checked itself for reason. It burned on its own fuel so that its size had no relation to its source ; we were often in a fever for something so trifling that we had forgotten it before it arrived. All day one would live in the sense of something to come ; it would be with one during lessons, bathing, digging, meals, until at last, getting into bed, one would notice it particularly and say : "But what am I expecting". Then one would discover that it had been doughnuts for tea, already eaten, but without any sense of fulfilment. The expectation had flowed over the fact as time runs over the apple flowers before one can grasp the spring. But with us, it was like an eddy on a strong tide. (p. 28)

The lyrical passages in the novel metaphorically suggest the creative nature of the imagination which throws up new vistas. Evelyn's mind strives to move out into unseen territories of novel impressions and ideas, but the pattern is not lost sight of. The reader comes across a remarkable passage somewhere in the middle of the novel, which will bear quoting in full, where a fresh vision supplied by the imagination is related to the familiar facts of life and the continuity of existence :

---

17. Paul Schilder, *Mind : Perception and Thought in Their Constructive Aspects* (New York, 1942), p. 179.

The mill stream running over the sluice through its channel of rough stone made a regular pattern at each side like a fan ; and in the middle where there was a post with runners for the sluice gates, a shape like the beginning of a four-in-hand cravat. Lower down the two side fans crossed over the middle stream so as to complete the tie. Two other fans sprang out here from two stone posts, set in the walls, and completed the pattern.

In daytime, when I wandered through the mill and the stream with my air-gun, I was apt to get no further than the bridge. I would even lie down and put my eye to the cracks between the boards in order to catch the water flying underneath. What fascinated me was the swift movement of the water and the regularity of the pattern. The water and the regularity of the pattern. The water flying over the smooth stone top of the fall was as bright as a melting icicle ; and so clear that the smallest blade of water-gross stirring within it could be seen as sharply defined as a specimen in ice ; it was disturbed only by the creasing of the water as it darted forwards, as if dragged by the weight of the fall. Then suddenly this bright sheet broke into spurts of foam against the bridge posts, and flying still more quickly, drew out, for ever new and for ever the same, the complicated fan pattern.

The edges of the different fan-shaped squirts of water were frilled with round work which reminded me of the crochet on Aunt Hersey's best tea-cloths ; but every form was perpetually active, jumping up and down, dancing on the glossy stream between the fans like a living creature. Every dancer performed his own extraordinary steps, whirling up, running round, tossing an arm or head right off into the air, and he was never actually in the line ; yet the whole long row was always one line, and it had been dancing like that, day and night, for nearly a hundred years. This, too, the sense of perpetuity fascinated into my feeling while I lay on the bridge, fascinated, and watched, for an hour at a time, the gentle waving of the emerald grasses within the calm, smooth water, the leap of the foam which always seemed about to break out from the pattern and never did so ; the careless variety of the dancer's invention (pp.153-4)

What is revealing is not only the sudden flash of an insight into an apparently common phenomenon but a perception of 'fixity in flux'. Gladys Risden, writing on 'Aesthetic experience in Childhood', explains and comments on the process :

> The organism's first impressions of any novel situation are chaotic and confused. Gradually the parts emerge from this confusion and relationship between parts become apparent. Throughout the process of emergence and establishment of relationships of parts, an organic whole is evolving. The whole of the organisms's previous continuity of experience has helped to determine his response at each point of the experience.[18]

Further on she writes :

> Throughout, the total organism will enter into the response—sense organs will be stimulated directly or indirectly, and brain centres will be organising these sensory elements into an integrated response that will involve every effector organ directly or indirectly.[19]

The child's response which help him to create fantasy out of different selections and continuations results in synaesthesia and the making of concretized imagery and conceit. These are illustrated in the description of Evelyn as he drifts in a boat on the sea :

> A sail in the scow, especially in high winds and rough weather, was like a battle, a series of battles ; a campaign carried on with the greatest possible violence and noise. The very memory of these roaring days defens my ears ; the continuous howling, like a distant angry crowd, of the wind

18. Gladys Risden, "Aesthetic Experience in Childhood", *Child Psychology*, ed., Charles E. Skinner and Philip Lawrence Harriman (New York, 1960), p. 307.

19. *Ibid.*

> in our thick shround ; the groans and shrieks of the spirit against the thick mast, in proportions resembling a carrot ; and the pumping of the mast itself in its iron ring, which was much too big for it, the loud creaks of the timbers which seemed ready not to fly but to rip themselves apart, the clangs and thumps of the anchor tumbling about in the bows among two or three empty buckets ; and above all, the ceaseless crashing, tearing, boiling, whistling, spitting, sobbing of the broken water through which we smashed out way, makes for the mind a sort of sea tunnel or hollow in the past when one stopps into a long green darkness of excitement and noise. (p. 115).

Synaesthesia or the mixing of the senses which occurs from an inability to distinguish one sense-impression from the other is a peculiar but natural trait of the child's mental make-up, as Alfred L. Baldwin explains :

> In addition to the differentiation of emotions, there is evidence that the senses—vision, hearing and the rest—are, in the young child, muchless distinguishable from one another than in adults. One phenomenon that has been found in some adults—*synaesthesia*—has been shown to be much more common in children.[20]

In prefatory Essay to this novel Cary, repudiating the criticism levelled against him that he divorced mind from body, imagination from sensory experience, writes imphatically that it is not so with him and that in the child the two parts, the senses and the imagination, can be functioning in isolation and at times in interplay.

The child imagination of Evelyn is thrilled by a lovely phenomenon, one of Nature's various moods and there is an irresistible desire in him to make an adventure. There is a mixed sensation of joy and terror :

---

20. Alfred L. Baldwin, *Behaviour and Development in Childhood* (New York, 1956), p. 91.

> On many of these summer nights, the sky, though it was free from cloud, was obscured by a special darkness. It was a very dark blue, in which the stars were almost imperceptible ; an immense but opaque dome full of blue darkness which seemed to tint the air itself. A night like this, hot and appressive and overcast, always excited us to feats of daring ; but it was also apt to frighten us. (p. 90)

Cary was alive to the sensations of the child like Wordsworth's boy who romped over the mountains like a roe haunted by 'the sounding cataract'. Cary has a brilliant passage on the sense-experience of the child :

> We were exploring the world, but only with our nerves. We had no words for classifying our discoveries. We were still like feelers, antennae of some larger being, the leaves of a sensitive plant, put out to examine the world. Our senses were still like a baby's hands which wave in the air at random until they strike against some cold or hot or wooly object, which may or may not create some interest in his mind.
>
> So we gathered sensations, smells, various excitements ; only now and then consolidated into an idea by an accident of attention, some remark. (p. 37)

In a world full of glow and beauty, the child builds up, in meaningful fragments, a moral world, circumscribed perhaps, but still there. The child imbibes the sense of evil, for example, from the dark waves of the sea through which he swam :

> I felt their evil ; their deadly quality, not aimed at me, but dangerous and teacherous in themselves. (p. 90)

Evelyn and Harry run through the heather and get the quiet of a soul :

> We travelled through this enormous and magnificent scene in tranquil happiness. We were tired from running about in the heather and already growing hungry we felt the nearness of supper, and bed, with that calm faith which

> belongs only to children and saints devoted to the love of God and sure of the delights of communing with him. (p 20)

The child is taught the Bible but dogma does not touch him as the essence of a religion is derived from the diversity of life and experience :

> It was an atmosphere much more truly religious than anything I have know since ; for it was of real purpose. We had our Bible lessons, of course, but the religion which actually stayed with us was something livelier, braver, keener than the church teaching ; and much more real. A lecture from a boy's parent, a sailor, about chasing slave shows in the Gulf, went to the bottom of our feelings at one flash. (p. 34)

All these moral glimmerings come to child in this tranquil flow of the memories of childhood through the mind of Evelyn corner. The world is no longer a moral experiment, darkly felt, as in *Charley is My Darling* but a moral testimony, happily got, of child-like conceptions of reality.

However skillfully Cary may have shown children and adults acting in close juxtra-position in the novel, the reader cannot fail to notice two separate worlds. The focus falls upon the attempt of the old tradition to draw the younger generation into its own fold. The drama of cross purposes is played out is an Irish family and the interplay of contrasted personalities is confined to this area of experience. The young Harry and Evelyn, aspirants to untrodden areas of magic splendour, are warned against precipitate action and assured of undisturbed peace in family life by their father. The ambitious young looking for new avenues of development and the complacent, tradition-bound and resisting father, together give a dramatic texture to the novel.

The desire to soar high into the air untrammelled by conventions is checked by Evelyn's father who, shrewd enough to keep the family running in its established tradition, takes care not to allow his son to wander away into the land of mysterious nothingness. His father's explanation of the cave associated with tradition is something of a grand puzzle to Evelyn, but he can interpret it from his own perspective :

> He was panting when he brought us into central chamber. There was tall peak of rock, an island, in the middle of this chamber. We could not reach this because to do so required a jump of five or six feet, impossible to my father with a child on his back. But he pointed to its high peak and to the dome of the roof, and said that it had fallen down perhaps a million years ago, "and there it's been in this hold, a long time before there were any people at all, or even fish".
>
> These words made me see the cave as not merely ancient, but different from any other, a survival from another world. The rocks which touched my bare ankle seemed so different from common rock that they had a special chill and sliminess, horrible and strange ; the dark green water, at which I gazed down best my father's shoulder, appeared strange even to the sight, a primitive water. I imagined that no fish could live in it. Above all, the light and noises in this cave seemed unique. (p. 39)

Pinto, the rebel artist, represents the new conscience as against Evelyn's father who has imbibed certain distinctive characteristics of the established tradition. Our impression of the novel as the conflict between the old and younger generation is confirmed by Cary's own explicit commentary :

> We were equally astonished by my father's compliments and by Pinto's surliness. We could not know that in my father's special politeness, we were seeing a last fragment of the eighteenth century ; perhaps the very bend and smile with which a gentleman of the grand tour saluted an artist, any painter, or actor or singer or ballerina ; and in Pinto, the first symptoms of the early twentieth, with its suspicious reaction from anything like a grand manner. (p. 186)

It is characteristic of Cary's impersonality that he does not emphasize the importance of one at the cost of the other. Evelyn in the novel synthesizes the two forces that counterbalance each other. He gives up his attempt at writing an epic and accepts his father's advocacy of poetry which makes 'living experience' a palpable reality :

> My epic, as I saw it last, in an old exercise book, when I cleared the attic, stopped in the middle of a line and had drawn over it, in blue chalk pencil, little crude sketches of diving men. Yet the quality of our living experience could be translated only into the experience of poetry which people would not read. They prefer, I suppose, to live it, if they live, in any true sense of the word, real lives ; and that is even easier today than it was when we were children. (p. 239)

The young Evelyn, lost always in the world of colourful imagination and strange nightmarish adventures, undergoes momentous experiences which show that the mind of Evelyn develops from the stage of instinctual pre-dominance into a consciousness of conceptual logic. A play written by Evelyn's elder brother Harry, dealing with the theme of freedom and enacted by the two brothers ends as a failure. The failure is an educative experience :

> We were not only ashamed and disappointed ; we had suffered a shock. Deeper than the sense of failure, there was the feeling that we had misunderstood the situation ; that plays were not so easy as they seemed. With this went, as always, the feeling that life, too, was not so easy as it seemed. (p. 175)

In the novel the child is shown as an individual. The self-identity is possible, as Cary himself puts it, 'as soon, however, as it begins to acquire knowledge, to reflect on it, to form ideas, it becomes a true individual soul. It can value the reality it knows, of a emotion. It can form moral ideas, it can face a moral situation, which is always unique, and decide upon its response. It is not only independent, but obliged to be so, and only a moral being, but a solitary person in a dangerous world of vicissitude'.[21] A similar view is taken by Marian E. Breckenridge and E. Lee Vincent : 'All sensitiveness to size, shape, colour, and the other properties of objects can be developed by good teaching into a source of genuine intellectual curiosity and into a widened aesthetic awareness which will be of value throughout life.[22] Although Evelyn's father is Cary's wise, socially conscious character who tries his level best to keep up the eighteenth century dignified life and also holds in check the ramifications of Pinto's anarchism into dangerous lines of thinking. Evelyn Corner in his passion for fresh visions harmonizes within himself child responses.

The novels of childhood, *Charley is My Darling* and *A House of Children* present the imaginative world of the child. This is a world which has its own values, tones and colours. The child dwells in it with imagination, sensation and what is significant in Cary, a moral sense. Much of Cary's views are corroborated as has been shown modestly in this chapter, by the findings of modern psychology. The child world is different from the adult world and there is always the tension between the child and the grown-up. The child descends into delinquency as in *Charley is My Darling* or rises to the rapture of a faith and understanding in *A House of Children*. Together, these novels give not only child experience in its sharpest contrasts and fluctuations, but also basic imagination of the child.

---

21. Joyce Cary, *Art and Reality*, Anchor Edition (New York, 1961), p. 25.

22. Marian E. Breckenridge and E. Lee Vincent, *Child Development* (Philadelphia, 1960), p. 367.

CHAPTER IV

Human Reality

Cary's major work is the first trilogy consisting of *Herself Surprised* (1941), *To Be a Pilgrim* (1942) and *The Horse's Mouth* (1944). They deal with the chaos of life, illogical and irrational, and it is the truthful presentation of these that gives the novel as a genre, its psychic substance or the 'liberated psychic substance in motion'.[1] *Madame Bovary* gives this movement of life uncontrolled by any sense of order or ideologue ; She just lives on by event and circumstance in the whirlpools of her passion and closes the tide of her life by taking poison *Anna Karenina* is similar because it deals with life and its unpredictability, its 'climactic curves leading to crises and conclusions'.[2]

Joyce Cary's *Herself Surprised* is a novel written in this order. It deals with reality, 'the reality which smashes every ideologue' for the subject 'is human nature, incessantly striving towards a personal achievement in a world which is essentially free and personal'.[3] Sara is the narrator. The purport of Cary was to emphasize character. He wrote :

> In life every richness of feeling and imagination intensifies the force of the person. But books are not life, they are limited by the character of the medium, the form

1. Nathalia Sarrante, "Flaubert", *Partisan Review*, xxxii, Number 2 (Spring 1966), p. 208.
2. Barbara Hardy, *The Appropriate Form* (London, 1964), p. 17.
3. Joyce Cary, *Art and Reality*, Anchor Edition (New York, 1961), p. 172.

of their expression. An in such a dilemma, whether to stick to my scheme, or to stick to character, the character as fell and known in the book, I stuck to my rule, which was character first.[4]

Sara unpretentiously was meant to be a cook. She had no doubts about it:

> It was true that I had come from a good home, for my father was a freeholder and working foreman, and my mother had been a teacher. I myself had prizes from school for recitation and scripture, and a certificate for sewing; and afterwards I had a very good training as kitchenmaid under a man cook in a good religious house with a very rich brewing family, who never allowed so much as an ounce of margarine or custard power or any made-up stuffs in their kitchen, even for the servants. My mother wanted me to be a first-class cook fit for the best service; and so did I. (p. 11)

Ironically, she is introduced into the artificial society of Mrs. Monday whose house 'was very pretty, too, all covered with trellis in front, for roses, and creeper behind'. (p. 12). In this home Matt pursued her. He used to wait for her in the back stairs and the attic landing. At first she resisted but he was insistent and bought her a ring. She felt transformed :

> In one week from that idle word my whole state was changed as much as if I had been made over into another woman. I could not believe it myself and still it seemed to me that I was play-acting, or that the world was more like a play than I had thought. (p. 16)

She marries him and works herself up into the grotesque. She dressed in a new pink which set tongues wagging that she was a common woman. She behaved atrociously.

> I tortured him so and suffered for him, but so it was.

4. Joyce Cary, Prefatory Essay to *Herself Surprised*, Carfax Edition (London, Reprinted 1960), pp. 7-8.

> It seemed I was two women ; and one of them a loving wife and the other mad and wicked. I did not know how to manage myself, any more than a filly feal running about the field with her tail in the air and pretending to bite the trees, and to kick at her own mother. (p. 20)

> She knew she was a fool and did him great harm. (p. 21)

She next became friendly with one Rozzie Balmforth, the bar maid who did a dirty trade. She introduced her to the Mondays. Foppishly dressed, Rozzie shocks Mr. Monday and her son by her lack of manners and crudity :

> "So you're another of them".
>
> "I beg your pardon", Matt said, all eagerness to make my friend welcome, especially because his mother and sister were looking at her already as if she was dirt on the carpet. (p. 18)

Rozzie knew she was all wrong : 'She looked bolder and fiercer than ever and fairly shouted at Matt : "I meant husbands, not pigs. I respect pigs". So then she turned to old Mrs. Monday without being introduced and gave here a note and said : "We know men, don't we, mam-hogs by night and monkeys by day". (p. 19)

Sara was full of the lusts of the flesh. She meets Hickson, a man of wealth and business. Se flirts with him and enjoys all the details of his attention.

> I did not know how I linked his pressing my arm especially where Maul might see, and saying that we would do so-and-so for Matt, who was worth ten of Hickson, in spite of his riches and cleverness. And then he began admiring my frock, which was a Russian blouse all ruffled down the front, lifting the fuffles and pretending to see how they were sewn to the bodice, but really to touch me. I did not think I liked it, and yet I thought, what harm if he enjoys it, poor little man. I owe a great deal to him, I thought, for he has got for me much I could never have got for myself. (pp. 27-8)

She went from bad to wrose in her intrigues. She has no qualms about it :

> If I went to the bad at last, it was not the fault of the times, but of myself. It was not because I loved the parties and the gaiety and even as a mother and a matron up in the thirties, danced through twenty pairs of shoes in a year ; but because I did not remember my weakness and study my faults, and because I forgave myself too easily for those evil deeds which always took me by surprise. (p. 36)

She next comes into contact with Jimson, a wayward artist, a character full of 'rumbustiousness contrifugal fertility'.[5] His wife is Nina, a simple and innocent girl. Sara realized her contrast with her :

> I don't think Nina ever cared much for me. That was natural ; for I was now getting full blown in the rushing tide of my worldly delights. Matt had given up trying to control my dress and Bradnall was used to it But when a little while ago I looked at cld photographs that Jimson had kept and saw the woman I was in my thirties and early forties, frilled and flounced and laced and thrusting myself in front and behind, I can't believe my eyes. There is no doubt that in those days I outdid Rozzie herself. I seemed a very bad kind of woman, worldly, common and worse. (p. 47)

It is Nina who gives her a flash back into the good life, mementarily felt perhaps : 'For Nina had great religious power so that though sometimes you hated her for her taking no notice of your troubles, the next moment she said something that went straight into you soul. She made you remember God and the shortness of your time on earth and your own littleness. (p. 56) She is impressed by Nina's love for Nature :

> For Nina, of course, trees and grass were holy. Indeed, I think everything was holy for her and I suppose, if God

5. Paul West, *The Modern Novel*, I, (London, 1965 edition), p. 112.

made the world, that she was right. But whether right or wrong, it was in her character and it made her different. And I looked forward now to my drive with here, for I thought: 'I've been getting too fond of my tea—I'm too fat too, which is just God's rightful, punishment for indulgence. It will do me good to see nature and enjoy it in spite of not having tea till five or even none at all. It's what I need, to clear all the rubbish off my soul'. (p. 55)

Sara now poses for the artist Jimson. She sits half-naked for a portrait. She is dizzy with excitement as he is wild with passion :

> Jimson was in his most outrageous spirits and I could see he wanted to flirt with me. He looked at me now with a different eye from the day before when he had drawn me. But, as I say, I was wild too, and I admit it, I did n't mind for anything, not even for his squeezing and pushing me on the stairs, or his risky jokes. I felt as I did with Rozzie and if he had asked me to drink in some public house, I might have done it, in spite of all Bradnall. (p. 60)

Jimson promises to marry Sara but is rilled with concupicence before marriage. Sara resists, at first, but succumbs lazily to the situation :

> I love the heat and lying in the sun and I know it makes me lazy and careless so I don't care what happens. So that my mind was laughing at little Jimson when he held my hand and told me he could make me so rich and give me furs and jewels ; yet my flesh delighted in his kindly thoughts. So it grew sleepy and I forgot myself and he had his way, yet not in luxury, but kindness, and God forgive me, it was only when I came to myself, cooling in the shadow, that I asked what I had done. Then, indeed, I felt the forebodings of my misery, and punishment, and I was weighed down all the evening. (pp. 92-3)

Once this happens it all becomes the inevitable :

> But though I jumped out of bed the next night when

> he came into me, I thought it was not worth while to keep what little decency was left me, and to deny him what he thought so much of. So I got back again to him, as sad and mild as any poor girl that has no right to her own flesh and let him do as he pleased. (p. 93)

Jimson is an isolated individual on acccount of his creative genius which receives unfavourable response from the community of which he is a member and his suppressed creativity explodes into acts of violence and lawlessness. He was always off in heated arguments. At Burnemouth he had a fight with a bus conductor in a public bar. (p. 97). He often pummelled and threshed Sara. Once blue and green with rage he shook her hands away from him and suddenly struck her. When she went upstairs her nose was bleeding and she had a blackeye. (p. 112). With all his riot, Gulley is a contrast to the prim Mondays. His artistic gift was his personal asset, while the Mondays were social parasites, ever worried about money. In Sara's movement from her husband's society into Gulley's company, Cary demonstrates the basic difference between the inner power that the artist possesses in spite of his outward coarseness and the social decorum which the Monday family maintains to commouflage its inward hollowness and the dearth of imagination. But Gulley suffers from the same disintegration as Sara does. He speaks of the need for absolute concentration on his painting, but the next moment he is at his wildest, raining several blows upon Sara's poor face. His beating of Sara who looks after his paintings and helps him financially has the same ironic stance. The comic portraiture of Gulley depersonalized between Sara and her friend Rozzie best illustrates the lost identify of the artist :

> There we were after supper in a little kind of sung behind the billiard-room, with some bottled beer Rozzie had got in from a public ; all of us in a row on an old horsehair sofa with its springs burst. First it was when the springs made noises under us that Rozzie made remarks, and do what I would, she set me off. Then Gulley was

such a queer sight, the little spindle, between us to big women, bulging out over him, that it made us laugh to see him. Rozzie would shoot me a glance over his bald head and roll her eyes over him with a face that made me laugh till I cried.

Then he, quick as he was, would chirrup 'Mahomed between the Mountains' or the 'Window's Cheese Mite' and Rozzie would fill up his glass and say: "You're getting warm, Mr. Rat—it must be the heat, I suppose", and "Take one, Mr. Gulley, your temperature's going up. Don't burst anything". (p. 83)

The heady affair set him taking in his comic vein :

He squeezed us by the arms and said : "The best paid in England and the finest four".

"Four", Rozzie said. "He's seeing things".

"I wish I could", he would say, for as I say, he had just caught Rozzie's note and, indeed, he always had that side to him. (p. 83)

Sara lived with Matt Monday as his wife, with Gulley as his concubine and now at the age of forty six goes to serve Wilcher, the lawyer, a chronic bachelor in London. There is a turn of the tide. At Tolbrook Manor, the home of Wilcher, where Sara resumes her cooking service, there is a fairer chance of her becoming her old self dedicated to service as symbolised by the kitchen :

... it seemed to me that it was providence Himself that had taken me by the hand and led me back to the kitchen. For where could a woman find a better life, I mean in a good house with a good draught in the chimney, and double sinks and really hot water, as I always had at Tolbrook. Then it came back to me about what poor Jimson had said about my true home being in a kitchen and that I was a born servant in my soul and my heart gave a turn over and I felt the true joy of my life as clear and strong as if the big round clock over the chimney-mouth was ticking inside me. (p. 149)

It is only when Sara is not allowed to work that one catches the irony. She gets into the muddle of a society where the master and the servant do not know where they stand. Wilcher goes against conventional propriety and bluntly proposes to Sara to sleep together.

Sara left Jimson. But his spell holds her. She suffers the contradictions of human nature and wants to return to him even after a three years' stay at Wilcher's house. This is one of life's paradoxes :

> I was terribly cast down, for I knew I would go back if he asked me, and he beaten and lose all my comforts. I dreaded it and yet I knew he had only to say the world. For cruel as he was, he had yet a hold on me. I don't know how it is but when you've lived with a man, and cooked and cleaned for mim nnd nursed him and been through troubles with him, he gets into your blood, whoever he is, and you can't get him out. (p. 166)

She veers to him, helping him with money in weekly instalments. She is not sure what she should do 'Whether to keep him in some comfort and please my conscience, or only to keep him away and please my flesh, I never could tell'. (p. 169). In order to pay off the colourman's bills for Jimson's paintings, she takes to cheating Wilcher, Cary gives through her as he does through the other too novels in the trilogy his 'vision of degradation and perversion of human life'.[6] Sara's consciousness makes her aware of her split personality :

> How I came into this double way of life, I cannot tell, except that I got used to my pickings ; and that I was bound to send something to Gulley ; and I had made an agreement with myself never to use my savings. (p. 183)

6. Golden L. Larsen, *op. cit.*, p. 112.

Sara is finally arrested on changes of stealing Wilcher's possessions over the years, old trinkets a gold watch, silver fruit knives, an ivory statue and two stamp albums. (p. 219). She is convicted and leaves Tolbrook House for prison. Cary with dexterity and insight, describes Sara's bewilderment at the adult level, recalling, in anti-thesis, the adolescent nightmare which Charley in *Charley is My Darling* suffered, as he was pushed into the police-car :

> So they sent for a cab to take me off to the station, I'll never forget Miss Clary's face when she came in and found a policeman in the kitchen and me mixing a salad, and Mrs. Loftus in the hall waiting for the cab. She could not believe her eyes or her ears.
>
> "What are you thinking of, Sara ? You're not going to let them take you before Uncle comes home". But I only shewed her the pie in the oven, not to leave it too long, and the cream for the custard. For I did not want to see Mr. W. then. I knew I was a guilty woman. I felt like the ghost of myself, just floating along in the draught from the stove to the sink and back again. I was not even afraid or unhappy. I was only surprised at myself and my devastations. (p. 218)

Cary is a novelist who has given us life in a flood. Sara strives to define herself, dissenting and acquiescing, as all the characters in the first trilogy do.[7] She always measures herself against a constant. That accounts for the several passages in the novel in which she recoils on herself to her own surprise. She sat for Jimson 'down to the waist'. Jimson painted her, humming and looking at her as if she had been a statue. Sara is amazed at her own reflection :

> It seemed to me then that I had been a fool to be so prim before and yet I wondered at myself. I could not tell whether I had done a religious thing or a bad one. When

7. Paul West, *op. cit.*, p. 112.

> I went home again, I was in wonder and dismay all the evening. I thought : 'What will I do next—there seems to be nothing I wouldn't do'. (p. 59)

Jimson kept on painting and tired would just fall beside her and snore. She marked how Jimson could be both wild and tame, uncommon and yet common :

> I was surprised but pleased, too. For it was as it should be. A honeymoon is one thing, and life is another. I was only surprised when I looked at it, because Jimson had turned so sensible and ordinary. (p. 101)

Wilcher was a character who deserved a better deal in spite of his weakness of the flesh. Sara knew she was unfair to him ; she essessed herself against an ideal code. She suffers qualms of conscience :

> Now although in the next years, I often suffered in conscience, and wondered at myself, while I walked in the gardens and thought : 'How is it that I can go about like this, like an ordinary person, and not be found out, or sink into the ground with shame ?' Yet the truth was that I was very happy. (p. 17ↄ)

She felt she could just be a cook ; her bane was her flesh. The novel ends with a significant reflection :

> A good cook will always find work, even without a character, and can get a new character in twelve months, and better herself, which, God helping me, I shall do, and keep a more watchful eye, next time, on my flesh, now I know it better. (p. 220)

There is a continuous relation going on in the character between the inner and outer side of human life. Cary described how great artists are concerned with this essential : 'So all great artists are preoccupied, as if by nature, with reality. They assume, from the beginning, that it is their task to reveal a truth about some permanent and fundamental real'.[8] It is this fundamental real which makes Charles G. Hoffmann describes Sara as 'the unchanging Eve'.[9] V.S. Pritchett reads the meaning into Sara's character and exaggerates the truth, as he is overwhelmed by it :

> Nature herself, unscrupulous, untidy ; and yet she is more than Nature of she has faith....she has a sort of soul which confidently, if deleteriously moves on in its earthly pilgrimage. The moving on is everything.[10]

In the case of Sara, the ideal consciousness does not determine the acts of the body. Sara thus lives and remains at a human level and never gets out of its reach. Cary's art consists in presenting this dark human landscape. This is the human reality at which he works in this novel and the other two novels in the trilogy.

The next novel *To Be a Pilgrim* (1942) is a complex work compared to *Herself Surprised* (1941). From Sara, the dominant character in *Herself Surprised*, we are taken to several characters in three generations of the Wilchers. The story is set back in time in nineteenth century England and moves on to the twentieth until the second world war. It covers a wide panorama of history. Wilcher of the first generation lived in a period when the Gladstone Government was in power. The span of history covers landmarks of history. There is the Jubilee year 1892 (p. 138), the Boer War 1900 (p. 153), the year of revolution 1906 (p. 182), the 1913 pre-war year (p. 220), the first world war 1914-18 when Tom Wilcher, the second son of the elder Wilcher, went to France in 1916 and was invalided out of the army in 1917. There is a reference to the armistice

8. Joyce Cary, *Art and Reality*, Anchor Edition (New York, 1961), p. 102.

9. Charles G. Hoffmann, "Joyce Cary and the Comic Mask", *Western Humanities Review*, xiii, No. 2 (Spring, 1959), p. 140.

10. Victor S. Pritchett, "Books in General", *New Statesman and Nation* (October 27, 1951), p. 464.

of 1919 (p. 255), the League of Nations (p. 247), the great strike (p. 336) and Hitler's rise to power and the Nazis in the Second World War. (p. 109, p. 223). More than these facts of history, the novel catches the elusive but palpable spirit of history from Alfred and Beowulf (p. 135) and 'British country gentlemen of the fourth century', to the nineteenth century when Tolbrook possessed a room of 'double refinement ; the Roman art of life, distilled through the long spiral of English Classicism'. (p. 128)

Cary deals, as a novelist does, not with history but the feel of history or the 'turmoil of change.[11] There is an advantage in this for history, like the arts, acts on life and displays 'an infinite variety and novelty of actual consequences'.[12]

The Wilcher family, a spreading tree, consists of the elder Wilcher, his wife, their three sons, Edward, Tom and Bill and a daughter, Lucy. The narration of the novel is done in reminiscence by Tom Wilcher when he is seventy-one years old. He is a 'man with a sense of history'[13] which makes him pivotal in this story which bobs up and down in the flux of Time.

Tom Wilcher was born in 1869 and recapitulates his family and his own life in 1939. He does this not in chronological sequence as in *Herself Surprised* but by flashback contract as Cary told John Burroughs and Alex Hamilton in an interview 'the chronological-run through by itself is no good.[14] He remembers his father the elder Wilcher, his mother, and his sister Lucy. In doing so he shows his father's affection and at the same time his adherence to an inflexible code governing his generation :

---

11. Joyce Cary, Prefatory Essay to *To Be a Pilgrim*, Carfax Edition (London, Reprinted 1959), p. 7.
12. Joyce Cary, *Art and Reality*, p. 159.
13. Andrew Wright, *op. cit.*, p. 120.
14. "Joyce Cary", An Interview conducted by John Burroughs and Alex Hamilton, *The Writer at Work*, ed., Malcolm Cowley (New York, 1956), p. 59.

> My father, unlike his daughter, could appreciate my mother's quality as well as Lucy's. His mind may have had an inflexible character, but his sympathies were pliant and comprehensive. He understood and valued my mother's peculiar sensibility and her gentleness of spirit, as well as Lucy's courage and passion. But coarseness and brutality in a woman was to him a sin against Nature, as well as his code. He thought of women as the guardians of a special virtue given them by God. If he had passed over Lucy's crime without the most determined punishment, he would have felt guilty before God, and even perhaps before some power more universal to his feeling : Nature. Lucy's crime was unnatural in a woman, and he beat her severely. (pp. 42-3)

Later in the novel, Lucy elopes and is married to the Benjamite Brown ; she leaves her husband in protest against his affair with a girl Ella. Brown later comes to take his wife back and behaves rather rudely with the elder Wilcher. Wilcher, enraged, asks Lucy to stay back out of her own free will. There is a schism in the character between his codified morality and his emotional liberalism :

> Our father had two contradictory views about women : one, that a wife must cleave to her husband at all costs ; the other, that a woman, as a living soul, should have all freedom. (p. 95)

Lucy is highly strong and emotional. Once when beaten by her father she tries to commit suicide by drowning :

> She was not even unconscious, and as soon as she had choked up the muddy water from her mouth, she began to kick and struggle, saying. "He can't hurt me—never—never".
>
> The gardener puzzled, I suppose, by this violence in a girl who had always appeared so sensible and dignified, set her down with a respectful gesture. *She ran at once*

back into the pond, but the man caught her before she was beyond her knees. (p. 45)

Lucy's faith in God is equally paradoxical as recorded by Tom Wilcher :

> The very idea of Lucy goes to my head. "There aren't such people now-a-day", I think. "And what if she had a devil. She did God's work. Out of devilry. She made something good and noble of her life". (p. 48)

Lucy runs away from her house and marries Brown a Benjamite. While she suffers and scrubs floors at the chapel in all humility and meekness, the irrational in Lucy's nature comes out in her brutal treatment of her husband as the narrative runs :

> Lucy was a terror to Brown ; she treated him often with such cruel and bitter contempt that he would howl to be delivered from her. She had brought him publicly to tears on more than one occasion. (p. 97)

Cary's point is that overemphasis on either the rationalizing intelligence or emotional excess shuts out the mind from apprehending the real. An abundance of feeling neutralizes the rational side in her. She gets so easily worked up over minor family matters that she exhibits her incapacity to understand the situation and goes so far as to accuse her most sensible mother of taking her son Robert to an unhealthy place :

> Amy, however, continued to take Francie to Hog Lane, And when Lucy abused her, in stratling language, she answered placidly, "It's not their fault they're dirty—they're that kind of people", as if speaking of some foreign race.
>
> "It is their fault. They're dregs. They wouldn't stay in Hog Lane if they weren't. It's just because they're dregs that mother kow-tows to them". (p. 217)

Cary refers in his *Art and Reality* to such 'man who are on the one hand emotional without sense and on the other full of the most rigid opinions on every possible subject without regard either to fact or sensibility'.[15]

Edward is Lucy's opposite in character. While Lucy is impulsive but illogical, Edward, the eldest son of Mrs. Wilcher, grows up into an astute politician on account of his sharp intelligence but suffers from an incapacity to gauge the feelings of others for he 'had not much penetration into character. He was too clever. He never understood the force of moral conviction in certain souls, or its variety of forms'. (p. 78). Julie, his mistress, complains of the absence of him of 'feelings for people, only for ideas'. (p. 201). He is too absorbed in political activities which deaden his sensitivity to aesthetic values. His ultimate defeat is ironically the cause of his over-reliance on political intelligence at the cost of his feeling self. His sudden decision to give up politics at a crucial moment in the National Movement of his country speaks of his fickleness and lack of moral courage. Tom pinpoints this major weakness of his brother and his mistresses :

> What was Edward's charm ; and Julia's and Mrs. Tirrit's ; so different in character ? A universal tolerance, based on a universal enjoyment. They were faithful to friendship, to kindness, to beauty : never to faith. They could not make the final sacrifice. They took a holiday at the wrong time ; or could not bother to keep up with the new arts ; or, like Mrs. Tirrit, did not face, in time, the doctor who would say, "You must have an operation". They would rather die in peace than live in pain. (p. 205)

In Tom Wilcher, the narrator of the novel, Cary dramatizes the confusion of values. There is little to doubt that Tom is faithful to the past. He speaks in his mother's bed room :

> But of course small-minded people hate what is rich to the mind. They hate the past, not because it is old, but because it might give them something new, something unexpected, and disturb their complacent littleness. (p. 32)

15. Joyce Cary, *Art and Reality*, p. 180.

The past is so ingrained in his mind that living as he does in the present, his memories 'like his bones, grow sharp with age and show their true shapes. The peace of the nursery, like all my peace, dissolves like the illusions of my flesh'. (p. 34). After the death of his father, the responsibility of running the family affairs falls upon Tom. While Edward swuanders away the family property and leads a care-free, licentious life, Tom remains committed to the established pattern. He seeks to check Edward, who revolts and wrenches himself from all restrictions and indulges in the new licence of the age by flirting with girls. Cary dramatizes the fundamental conflict between the claims of tradition and that of revolution. Temporarily under the influence of his brother Tom plunges himself into the rising tide of nationalism during the First World War. But, ironically, Tom, instead of enjoying mental peace, is shocked to see the fire of revolution, set ablaze by Edward and himself, which now threatens to consume the very system he is so eager to preserve :

> The cloth caps came to Parliament in 1906, and their cry was not for eternal life and the judgment of God, but for the world's life and justice on earth. A revolution deeper than the French. Rousseau said, 'Trust human nature to do the right thing'. But now they say, 'By our will be shall remake the world, and humanity also".

> The blue shadows had stretched across the fields and were rising up the front of the house until nothing was left except the golden chimney posts against a sky as dark as a lawyer's blue bag. "It is like a Christmas card", I thought, "except that it is real and I am seeing it, and it is far more beautiful than any picture. Because it is real, and so it must die. It is dying so fast that I can hardly bear to look at it". (p. 199)

Cary sees this split self in Tom when he calls his 'liberal by conviction but conservative in heart. In him, that is, the attachments of sentiment, which, are the perpetual root of conservative feeling, are stronger than the drive to adventure'.[16] He can appreciate the change but cannot jerk himself out of the past : 'We can understand new ideas in the world, but we cannot share new feelings'. (p. 283)

His relations with Lucy, his sister, is both a joy and a terror to him. As a child he is 'happy with Lucy because all about was a familiar world, not escecially friendly to me, but understood'. (p. 26). Later, the sight of the same Lucy found living a hard, tortuous life in the dirty surroundings of the Benjamites sickens his nerves.

Tom Wilcher, apprehensive of public scandal, is opposed to Edward's connection with Julie, a civilised and intellectually alert lady and succeeds in breaking the relationship, but finds himself involved with her. That is association with Julie is the result of his divided mind becomes clear when the Lady's proposal of marriage shakes him out of a delusion into a consciousness of his position in Tolbrook which symbolizes the old convention :

> My conduct may seem absurd and even pusillanimous. I can't explain even now why I felt so convinced that it was impossible to marry my mistress. But I have this excuse, that by this time, Tolbrook had come almost entirely into my possession. It was saved. And I felt perhaps that to bring a Julie to Tolbrook would be an impiety to my father's house, now in my case. (p. 209)

Wilcher's split personality further manifests itself in money matters. He shows obsessive interest in money which 'enters into the whole fabric of society. Nobody attends to it, any more than they trouble about their own blood, until it runs thin or does not run at all'. (p. 182). Money, for Wilcher, becomes at once an instrument of self-interest and service to others. While he takes secret pride in having Tolbrook under his possession, he offers financial assistance to Amy on purely selfless grounds, after her husband's death :

16. Joyce Cary, Prefatory Essay to *To Be a Pilgrim*, Carfax Edition (London, Reprinted 1959), p. 7.

> Bill died suddenly three weeks later.
>
> But Amy would not accept the money, even on the most business like terms. She said in effect : "If I borrowed all this money from you I'd never know how I was going to pay it back".
>
> I accused her of being too particular, and we had a little argument. For Amy was an obstinate woman. "A sister", I said, "should not object to being under a small obligation to a brother". (p. 261)

Against this human attitude, Tom's angry outburst against Robert and Ann for their coal, commonsense approach to money extends his schizophrenia to comic proportions :

> "I see you think I am a kind of moral idiot", I said to the children, to all our surprise. For all at once I had lost my temper. "An old mister who can only think and talk about money and shake his will every time that he's crossed. But it's you who are the idiots, yes, perfect idiots—not to know that money is important—extremely important. I've had to do with money all my life, and I fell you that it's not only the root of evil, but the root of good, too", etc., and so on. (pp. 181-2)

Wilcher's position is really ambivalent. He is a trained lawyer expert at unravelling the tangled knots of the Law, but it is difficult to account for his naive submission to the outworn codes of conduct of his society.

Tom Wilcher, undoubtedly, stands out a complex character and as Orville Prescott observes, 'one of the most substly developed, complete and original characters in modern fiction.[17] Walter Allen has a like perception, Wilcher is a true original : there is no other character like him in the range of our fiction.[18]

17. Orville Prescott, "Two Modern Masters : Cozzens, Cary", *In My Opinion : An inquiry into the Contemporary Novel* (New York, 1952), p. 169.

18. Walter Allen, *Joyce Cary* (London, Revised Edition 1963), p. 2.

Wilcher fascinated Charles G. Hoffmann on account of his capacity to get across to the reader the essential meaning of the trilogy more coherently and convincingly than either Sara Monday or Gulley Jimson could do.[19]

The centre of vision in the novel is Wilcher himself and his character is dramatized. V.S. Pritchett praises the novel for 'the intricacy of reflected points of view.[20] The complicated stories are organically related and since Cary's method keeps the author out what we get is life-content and not didacticism, 'the sense of life, of human complexity ; such a sense educated more than overt moralizing'.[21]

The elder Wilcher wavers between his tender affection for children and his rigid code of conduct. Lucy is a protestant and has faith in God but she is over emotional and cannot understand human situations. Edward, a spirited revolutionary, lacks the warmth of feeling. Tom Wilcher escillates between tradition and revolution, convention and change, self-interest and his sense of duty.

Besides these mercurial and fluctuating characters, there are the norms of human reality or characters of integrity with a social purpose. They are the fixities or constants which help us to measure the obliquities of the aberrants in the novel. Mrs. Wilcher in *To Be a Pilgrim* is the first character in the Wilcher family retaining the classical dignity of service and the strength of soul, with a highly developed social consciousness among her own husband and children. Tom Wilcher depicts her endearingly getting behind the veil of her character :

> I did not perceive for many years the long slow tragedy of a women, obliged to accept the niche that her children, thoughtless enough, had made for her ; and to live in it, as life prisoners live in a call. But that, I dare say, is the

19. Charles G. Hoffmann, *op. cit.*, pp. 139-142.
20. V.S. Pritchett, *op. cit.*, p. 464.
21. Paul West, *The Modern Novel* (London, 1963), p. 42.

> common fate of women like my mother, whose very love makes them feel guilty, because they could never satisfy its demands, whose pride of soul prevents them from complaint or self-pity. They are, I daresay, the prodest and the humblest of creatures ; the most lonely and the most self-reliant. To her dying day, my mother discharged those duties which she had laid upon herself : visits, a correspondence which often kept her up half the night ; personal charities, the accounts which were always wrongly added. I do not suppose she thought of herself as an unlucky woman, who had married the wrong man, and had a family as strange to her breeding, as young wild cats to a Persian. (p. 267-8)

The elder Wilcher particular about 'rules of conduct, carefully and justly administered' (p. 29) and lacking in the loving kindness, emotional warmth and the delicate sensibility of his wife, thinks of womankind through her : 'He looked in women, above all for that peculiar grace which inspired all my mother's acts and moods ; a grace of spirit as well as body ; a charity of soul which effected even her carriage and her voice'. (p. 42) Tom remembers his mother's goodness and the impression she made on him as a child. Even the room once occupied by her breathes the air of her character and gives a spiritual thrill to him :

> I seemed in that room to be existing within my mother's being, an essential quality, indescribable to me then, and not easy to describe now ; something that was more grace than happiness, more beauty than joy, more patience than rest, dignity without pride, a peace both withdrawn and sensitive. But for me, as a child, beauty, grace and distinction. Even young children understand and love distinction of the soul, because it speaks from mind to mind, and gives, them confidence in the world. (p. 31)

She had purpose ; she had stability. She was no fallen leaf of a tree blown about by the winds of chance. She did not suffer the besetting folly of modern times described by Arthur E. Morgan in his book *Search for Purpose* :

> One of the tragedies of life is the large number of people who have not found anything significant to do with their lives, and who try to fill them with "busy-work". This purposelessness is not due primarily to genetic limitation, but to the fact that many men have not yet become infected with they concept and spirit of conscious purposefulness.[22]

Mrs. Wilcher's son Bill and his wife Amy live a life of constancy while others vacillate :

> Bill and Amy had the unbreakable faith of children who come home every day to a new world ; and from that faith, they looked out, as monks once looked from this room, at the world as a spectacle. They did not need to think of themselves, for they knew exactly their purpose and their due. So, even on the last day of his leave, Bill spent half the night mending his mother's work-box, and Amy did not protest. (p. 106)

Both Bill and Amy possess an integrated personality in which inner goodness, social instinct and practical wisdom are harmonized. Bill has inherited his mother's high-mindedness. He is fatelly stricken with cancer. On his death-bed he talks to his brother Tom about his unfinished garden and what it meant to him :

> And I still do not know what had suddenly made me feel small and mean beside the improvident Bill with his absurd passion for a small garden. My wonder at the improvidence remained, but it was thrust aside by the sense that to Bill dying, a few trees, flowers, etc., planted and established by himself : a view opened, might have a special value and importance.
>
> Bill himself showed no change of mood. He said in the same detached tone : "It would be a good spec". And then, as if asking for my approval : "The idea is, you come

---

22. Arthur E. Morgan, *Search for Purpose* (Chio, U.S.A., 1955), pp. 188-9.

down here on a hot day and have tea under the new willow and you'll have the view in front of you all the time. My idea is that you need two or three different tea places in a garden".

"A very good idea. A splendid idea". (p. 260)

The garden is the concretilization of Bill's feeling for the comfort of others, skin to Mrs. Wilcher's wider and deeper sense and opposed to Tom's intellectualized view of sacrifice.

Ann represents the modern generation. She is a doctor and looks after her uncle Tom Wilcher who is suffering from a bad heart. Wilcher sums up her character :

> Ann suddenly appeared from the garden to ask me if I wanted tea. And as she seemed in very good spirits, I asked her if it was wise for her to be out in such a wind. "It's not me but you", she answered. "How is the enemy behaving" ? meaning my heart.
>
> She then took my pulse and sent me to bed, saying that I had throughly upset myself. I obeyed without protest. For I still felt guilty before her. It is always dangerous to forget that in every human soul, however irreligious and irresponsible, God has planted some spark of altruism, some kind and unselfish feeling. I believe Ann to be, at bottom, a good creature, spoilt only by a bad education. (p. 92)

Ann's love for the past is not just sentimental but has an academic seriousness about it. Tom comments on the new look which Ann has given to the room of Edward, her father :

> It gave me great pleasure to see this beautiful and dignified room, restored to use and life. It was a room which, unlike Julie's spoke of courage and enterprise. The strange but brilliant pictures, which still gave me a certain discomfort, the strong colour and bold decoration, the solid furniture and noble books, both from the most manly and lively century of our history, these were an inspiration.

> They said, "This is a place not for retirement but for counsel with strong minds : and meditation upon great examples". But a keener pleasure was to see Edward's daughter, in his own armchair, sitting at home once more among his own possessions, so piously gathered by her energy. (p. 237)

Ann is accused of having a 'cold, clinical attitude'[23] towards her husband, Robert, an engineer. We are told that both fall in love with each other and get married. It is true that the quickness of their marriage is matched by the amazing alacrity with which they drift apart and leave Tolbrook on separate adventures. The Ann-Robert relationship would seem to emphasize the uncompromising egotism of the present generation. But a careful study of the novel reveals that this emotional imbalance of Ann is only a temporary aberration. She acquires understanding, sobers up through her study of the past history and goes out in search of Robbert. The two become units, come back to the old house and settle down to a quiet conjugal life devoted to their respective professions.

Tolbrook is the repository of life's values for Wilcher. His wanderings till he meets Sara and is rejected by her reflect his frantic search for a fixed ground to stand on, which is ultimately possible when he is caught by Robbert and Ann and taken back to Tolbrook. His soul-killing despair turns into hope : "To and old man who has admitted that he is finished, the years, fly, but each day is a gift of heaven. To streaming windows, he says, "Once more I see the beauty of your melting lights and hear an English shower". He greets each spring and harvest as a piece of good luck". (p. 324). He realizes that he cannot find solace in escapism and he had to surrender before the kind-hearted Ann 'because I cannot fight and now it seems to me that not change but life has lifted me and carried me forward on the stream. It is but a new life which flows through the old house ; and like all life, part of that sustaining power which is the oldest thing in the world'. (p. 328). Tom's faith is revived and from confusion and ambivalence he moves on to a sense of

23. Charles G. Hoffmann, *op. cit.*, p. 141.

purpose which marked the lives of this mother, his brother Bill and his neice Ann.

Cary wrote : 'So, too, human nature and its social relations present certain constants'.[24] This is precisely what Cary tries to bring out in this novel. The constants emerge, not as in a novel of ideals, but like flowers plants struggling and thrusting their heads through the tangle of brambles and thorns which seek to choke them. The good comes out in a paradox as Cary wrote : "man is condemned to be a pilgrim in an unexplored wilderness'.[25] The pilgrim sense occurs in the novel at different points as positive assertions. Wilcher wrote to Sara at night :

> "We are the pilgrims who must sleep every night beneath a new sky, for either we go forward to the new camp, or the whirling earth carries us backwards to one behind. There is no choice but to move, forwards or backwards. Forward to the clean hut, or backward to the old camp, fouled every day by the passers", etc. (p. 37)

The pilgrim is on a quest. Children do so in their own naive way :

> The young are born pilgrims. Babies, as soon as they can walk, begin to explore the world. As every nurse knows, their first idea is to escape from their keepers. They are free born and look upon the whole earth as their possession. To be free is to be young. (p. 301)

To Wilcher, with all his education and protestant evangelism, life is a serious of disillusionment and dark disappointments : 'that all the schemes of politicians, with their promises of security ; all the near paradises of the churches, are fraud or delusion. The best that can be hoped from any government is that it will navigate among unknown rocks and unexpected hurricanes without sinking the ship and drowning the crew'.[26]

---

24. Joyce Cary, *Art and Reality*, p. 19.
25. Joyce Cary, Prefatory Essay to *To Be a Pilgrim*, p. 7.
26. *Ibid*, pp. 7-8.

The pilgrim should find his way yet there is not much he can do about it, caught as he is, in the worldly and the mechanical. Wilcher ruminates :

> A pilgrim is not a lost soul, I thought, nor a wanderer. He is not a tramp. But these are lost souls who don't even know that they are lost. They read three newspapers a day saying different things, and then they put on their black overcoats and hats and come to some place like this, to look at each other's hats and coats and to feel nothing, to say nothing, to think nothing, only to wait. (p. 313)

The malady is not of the young only but of England as a whole. There is a decline in civilization and an all-round collapse :

> I thought I could be an adventurer like Lucy and Edward ; a missionary. I shouted the pilgrim's cry, democracy, liberty, and so forth, but I was a pilgrim only by race. England took me with her on a few stages of her journey. Because she could not help it. She, poor thing, was born upon the road, and lives in such a dust of travel that she never knows where she is.

"Where away England, steersman answer me ? We cannot tell. For we are all at sea". (pp. 341 2)

The crisis notwithstanding there is hope and faith. There are inspired utterances and apprehensions of the transcendental and the immanent :

> As I say this, I feel the very presence of God, not only within me, but in the whole surrounding air, as love, friendship, beauty, so that it is as if these feelings existed not only within me but in the nature of things ; as if the mountains, the clear sky, the little fields below, my friends, were bound together not by my feelings about them but by a reciprocal character of delight and understanding. I think I know what it means to have perfect faith ; and as I turn again to climb, I perceive that I belong to God. (p. 141)

As Wilcher watches the trees, the limetree, the best of them all, he passes from sensation to thought and mysticism :

> The organ noise of bees, like vox angelica, the scent which made the blood race, the slow smooth fall of light in its thousand rills, over the living flesh of this beautiful and secret creature, entired at once the eyes and the imagination. Within that burning free I felt God's presence. And there I bathed in an essence of eternity. (p. 221)

To Be a Pilgrim thus, in extraordinary subtlety, mingles permanence with change, security with insecurity, generation set against generation or humanity in social reality, even as *Herself Surprised* deals with humanity in individual reality.

The final book in this remarkable trilogy is *The Horse's Mouth* (1944), a book in which he mingles the individual with the social through the anarchist Gulley Jimson. The story is of his adventures in art and life. Cary describes it as a comedy of facetiousness. There is a tragic under-current beneath a surface sangfroid and the burlesque. Cary writes about this :

> Any one who has served in a war knows the man who is suddenly full of jokes on the night before an attack, even just before going over the top.[27]

Cary applies this psychological situation to Gulley and elaborates this in an excellent passage :

> Jimson, as an original artist, is always going over the top into No Man's Land, and knows that he will probably get nothing for his pains and enterprise but a bee-swarm of bullets, death in frustration, and an unmarked grave. He makes a joke of life because he dare not take it seriously.[28]

The novel opens with Jimson, just out of prison, rejoicing in Nature's bewitching loveliness and pouring forth his lyrical sentiments in an impressionistic vein :

---

27. Joyce Cary, Prefatory Essay to *The Horse's Mouth*, Carfax Edition (London, Reprinted 1961), p. 7.

28. *Ibid*

> I was walking by the Thames. Half-past morning on an autumn day. Sun in a mist. Like an orange in a fried fish shop. All bright below. Low tide, dusty water and a crooked bar of straw, chicken-boxes, dirt and oil from mud to mud. Like a viper swimming in skim milk. The old serpent, symbol of nature and love. (p. 11)

He walks straight into his studio, a boat-house where he painted. The moment he sees his half-finished picture, his imagination sets to work on the creative possibilities :

> The serpent wants to be a bit thicker, and I could bring his tail round to make a nice curl over the tree. Adam is a bit too blue, and Eve could be redder—to bring up the blues. Yes, yes, I thought, getting a bit excited, as I always do when I come back to work after a holiday, I've got something there. Adam's right leg is a gift, whatever you may say. Nobody has done that before with a leg. What a shape. I must have been tight or walking in my sleep when I knocked that off. And yet it's leggy all right. If that limb could speak, it would say, 'I walk for you, I run for you, I kneel for you. But I have my self-respect'. (p. 15)

Jimson cracks jokes with Nosy, a small boy interested in painting, who, out of sympathy for the artist with non to look after him, brings him tea and something to eat in spite of his mother's repugnance for those who paint. Left alone, Jimson is obsessed with his painting :

> Yes, I thought, but the trouble about a leg like that, it sticks out. It's like a trumpet in the violine and a trumpet doesn't mean anything by itself. Any more than a sneeze under the stage. And if I work any brass into the top left-hand corner, it will have to go into the right bottom corner as well, into Eve, in fact, and she'll come right out of the canvas into the stalks. Only way to hold her down would be to make the serpent's head scarlet. (p. 16)

Gulley Jimson is on a career of hood-winking and cheating. He tries to establish his fame to Hisckson, an art dealer, in a pretentious way :

> Just then I found myself in a telephone box. Habit, I suppose. I never pass an empty telephone box without going in to press Button B. Button B has often been kind to me. It didn't give out anything this time, except an idea. I had some coppers, so I rang up Portland Place. Put a pencil between my teeth, and asked for Mr. Hickson. The young butler answered in his voice like a capon's crow, "Who shall I say ?" "The President of the Royal Academy". "Certainly, Sir, please hold the line". Then Hickson droned at me like a bankrupt dentist with toothache, "Mr. Hickson speaking". I kept the pencil well in front and gobbled. "Mr. Hickson, I understand you possess nineteen canvasses and about three hundred drawings by the celebrated Gulley Jimson". (pp. 16-7)

He keeps up the ruse of being an eminent artist with one Captain Jones :

> "Excuse me, Captain ?" "Yes", And I told him about the William Blake Memorial Association. I had been secretary of this Association for six months. Objects : to buy Blake's house in London. Hang originals on the walls. And have a caretaker to show the stuff and explain all about it. The idea was to charge six pence a visitor. A hundred visitors a day would make two thousand a year. (pp. 22-3)

Later, he visits Hickson's house with the barmaid Coker and there looking around, he filches things. Hickson's servant observed the theft whispered the same in Hickson's ear who, pretending to go outside, rang up the police. Gulley was beyed. He tried to run but before that, was caught by the Policemen :

> I'm sixty-seven, but I'm light and I can still run. I might have beaten that copper if he hadn't blown his whistle. But then coppers started up all round me. They

> seemed to come out of the street gratings, and drop from the sky. And they all took hold of me at once and nearly pulled my arms off.
>
> "That's enough", I said. "Be careful what you're doing. I'm Mister Gulley Jimson, and I shall put this matter into my lawyer's hands. First-class lawyers. For false imprisonment and assault. Obviously you don't know who I am. Call is taxi". (pp. 109-110)

Gulley tries to sell shady pictures. He edges into a customer and tries to dupe him into striking a sale :

> And as Nosy went into a paper shop, I said to the young duke, "Excuse me, Sir, but are you interested in art. I have here, at a great reduction, some of the finest reproductions of the photographic science. In plain envelope. Studies for students. Passed by censor. Latest lighting effects. For adults only. Half a guinea".
>
> "That's all right, old man", he said, "I was looking for you. Just step in here". And he took me by the arms and pushed me up an alley. "Fact is" he said, "I've had a complaint".
>
> "Have you ?" I said. "Well, look here". And I opened an envelope and showed him my cards. Two local churches and a sunset over the sea. "What's wrong with that ?"
>
> "Just what they told me", he said. "Why", he said, taking me by the neck and giving me a poke in the stomach with his knee that nearly broke me in two. "You dirty old crook—You son of a louse. What do you mean coming here on my pitch and swindling decent people with your filthy tricks". (p. 228)

Gulley is in need of money. He Walks with Sara and in a conversation finds out that his painting is kept by Sara to be sold to some dealer to cover her funeral expenses. He finds out that the painting is in Byles's chest and Byles is in hospital.

This effects his *mens rea* and he goes to buy an iron piece to open the chest :

> I stopped only at the ironmongers to get a box-opener. And I was in the flat quicker than I had expected. But just as I worked the crow into Byles's chest, Sara put her head round the door. She had followed me home. Just like Sara to suspect me. And before I could creep under the bed she saw me and rushed down the passage, screaming "Police".
>
> I got a big fright. I didn't want the police. It might have meant five years. And five years would have finished me. I ran after Sara and grabbed her by the back of her skirt. But she still kept on screaming "Police". So I gave her a little tap on the bonnet with the Iron Duke, to restore her to her senses ; and a little push away from the window. Whereupon she fell down the cellar stairs into some dark hold. (pp. 262-3)

Gulley was now sixty-seven years of age and Time had told on him as it did on Sara. She was now a shrewder person than before. Once when they met, Gulley wanted her to part with the Jimson paintings in her possession. The thrust and parry between them was engaging, a battle of sly wits :

> "Come, Sara, you've had a good innings—You've squeezed the lemon. Three husbands and five children—not counting the stand-ins, the Freds and the Dickies—it's a lot of happiness for one woman".
>
> "Don't talk of happiness like that, Gulley, as if it was all over. I never was happy unless I was with you, and you gave me a chance. I always say there was no one like you for gaiety. Oh dear, when I saw you on that Wednessday, it did bring back the old times, and what times they were". And there she was looking at me as if she could eat me without sauce, the old crocodile. I've set the tow slight in the old cask. I thought, It's the last flare of the old bonfire ; and there may be a lot of combustible there

> still. You can't tell by the bung, I'll get my face singed unless I'm careful. (p. 79)

The hectic life of Sara and Gulley in *Herself Surprised* is turned to a memory in a typical Gulley manner :

> For the truth was I was a bit excited. I'd forgotten what Sara was like. The real Sara. The old individual geyser. And she'd gone a bit to my head. (p. 41)

On another occasion it is Sara who remembers the past from her side :

> "Come on, Sall", I said. "Get up, old lady". For I thought she would dissolve away on the pavement.
>
> "Yes, I thank God for it. We've got something better than noses, haven't we. We've got our memories and they last better than any nasty flesh". (p. 85)

He remembers the bat pictures where Sara figured his blood tingling as he sketched her :

> Yes, I found out how to get Sara on the convas. Some of her, anyhow. And I was always at her, one way or another. The flesh was made word ; every day. Till he, that is Gulley Jimson, became a bleeding youth. And she, that is, Sara, becomes a virgin bright. (p. 52)

Sara comes in and out of his life in this novel but there was more in life than just her. There was Coker, the bar-maid, and Mrs. Coker a nagging woman. Gulley, homeless and destitute, stayed with them for a while. He once tried to beat Coker but got a severe one instead. The incident is narrated by Gulley :

> But the only time I ever tried to give Coker a slap—and that was under provocation—she got in first with a clump which blacked my eye and nearly broke my jaw. And then kicked me downstairs. In the proper style. It's not really a kick when done by an expert. It's a punch with the foot. And the foot applied rather high on the crack. Coker

> shot me off the top step like a rocket, and I had so many bruises on me I couldn't take my trousers off or put my boots on or scratch the back of my neck, for a fortnight. It makes me laugh to think of it. (p. 30)

Gulley's relation with the Cokers suffered a rude shock. His painting of The Fall on which he had set his heart received an ignorminous and at the hands of Mrs. Coker. He came to her to collect his picture and is told by Coker, the barmaid, what Mrs. Coker did with it. The effect to Gulley is like the end of the world :

> "She cut it up and mended roof with it. Why, didn't you notice—".
>
> I looked up to listen. And you could hear the rain rattling on the canvas like shot on a drum.
>
> "You know how the boards used to leak", said Cokey, "but of course she had to have the canvas tarred over—it's made a lovely job".
>
> I felt as if the top of my skull was floating off. I was quite feeble. To lose the Fall like this, suddenly, it was like being told your home and family had fallen down a hole in the ground. (p. 167)

Life was at cross-purposes with Gulley. He was confronted with two worlds, that of the new emergences with their dubiousness, and his own dormant within himself. He suffered the changes he observed around him :

> It was the Church against Darwin, the old Lords against the Radicals. And I was the battleground. (p. 62)

Gulley was cynical about Governments and found them little else than red tape and travesty. He once told the boy Nosy, in his radical manner :

> What is a government, Nosy ? It's a committee of committees and a committee hasn't even got trousers. It's only got a typist, and she's thinking of her young man and

next Saturday afternoon at the pictures. If you gave a government imagination, it wouldn't know where to put it. It would pass it on to the cat or leave it out for the charwoman to be taken away with the tea leaves. The only good government", I said, "is a bad one in the hell of a fright; yes, what you want to do with government is to put a bomb under it every ten minutes and blow its whiskers off—I mean its sub-committees. (pp. 217-8)

Jimson is a rebel not only against society, but art as well. He sharply reacts against the old schools :

Good-bye impressionism, anarchism, nihilism, Darwinism, and the giddy goat, now staggering with rheumatism... And I studied Blake and Persian carpets and Raphael's cartoons and took to painting walls.

But I rubbed most of them out again. They looked like bad imitations of the old masters ; or made-up, pompous stuff. They didn't belong to the world I lived in. A new world with a new formal character. (p. 64)

There is a conversation between Sir William Beeder and Gulley on the French Impressionists like Manet and Monet. Sir William says that the greatness of the French Impressionists is due to their rejection of classical rules. Gulley gives a vitriolic reply :

"Oh Lord", I said. "Listen to them". Oh God, these poor dears—and didn't Manet and Monet talk about their theories of art until the sky rained pink tears and the grass turned purple—didn't Pissarro chop the trees into little bits of glass. And Seurat put his poor old mother through the sausage machine and roll her into linoleum. (p. 153)

Jimson has to live in a society which is not favourable to art. His advice to the boy Nosy, who is interested in art, not to take to this line has sarcastic overtones :

"But you're not working. You're thinking about art. Now look here, Nosy, you're on the road to ruin. Do you want to break your mother's heart, and your wife's heart, and your children's hearts, unless they're all bastards and stand on their own feet. I know what I'm talking about. My son Tommy was a scholarship boy—went to Oxford, and now he's a gentleman. A real gentleman with Christian feelings and a sense of responsibility and hand-made shoes. And born in the Institution. And how did he do it ? From sticking to the books. And what you think would have happened to Tommy if he'd begun to play around with all this art nonesense. I told him. I said, 'If I catch you drawing or painting, Tommy, I'll skin you with a blunt rake. Art and religion and drink. All of them ruin to a poor lad. Leave'em to the millionaries that can afford to go to the devil first-class all the way. You've got to work for your living'. (pp. 44-5)

Gulley's apathy to art was from his earliest years. Cary remembers his father who is the origin of this character :

Gulley's old father in this book is taken from life and I, as a boy playing with paint in school holidays, remember very well the feelings of pity and surprise with which I looked at a gilt-framed cancas which he had brought out to show me, and propped against an apple tree among the weeds and cabbage stalks of a Normandy farm garden. I have an idea that it had just come back to him, rejected by the Academy which ten years before had been glad to hang his works.[29]

Gulley himself in the novel has a characteristic passage which well fits in with Cary's own father :

I couldn't forget seeing my father, a little grey beared old man, crying one day in the garden. I don't know why he was crying. He had a letter in his hand ; perhaps it was to tell him that the Academy had thrown out three more Jimson girls in three more Jimson garden. (p. 61)

---

29. pp. 9-10.

Lack of social understanding and harmony results in Jimson's psychic tension. In his confused state his faith in art seems to falter, even though temporarily, 'But I felt so old I wondered how my legs kept hanging on to my body. And I couldn't even think of what to do with the blank canvas. My eyes were dead as code and my ears only heard noises'. (p. 57). Jimson's consciousness of his plight fills him with a sense of loneliness :

> And to-night it seems that I can't paint at all. I've lost sight of the maiden altogether. I wander weeping far away, until some other take me in. The police. It's quite time. I'm getting too old for this rackety life. (p. 65)

There is a deeply moving self-revelation of the artists depression born of social inhibitions in the free exercise of the individual imagination :

> I should have liked to take myself in both hands and pull myself apart. To spite my guts for being Gulley Jimson, who, at sixty-seven years of age, after forty-five years of experience, could be put off his intentions, thoroughly bamboozled and floored, by a sprout of dogma, a blind shepherd, a vegetated eye, a puffed-up adder of moralities. (p. 51)

Lack of communication leads to the rupture in human relations. Jimson is describing a scene where people living in the same house are unable to transcend their narrowness and threat each other as sworn enemies :

> And we came into the kitchen where about fifteen chaps were eating, each trying to turn his back on all the others at once ; and to cover his plate. For to have anyone look on your food in a common ledging-house kitchen is a misfortune. The envious eye makes you forget the taste even of Wiltshire ham. And the critical eye which is the evil eye turns a cheap kipper into sulphuric acid and old leather. (p. 138)

Jimson suffers the decrepitude of age and the limitations which that and art put on him. It is a sorry spectacle of Jimson viewing a natural scence and is unable to put it on canvas :

> Sun coming up along a cloud bank like clinkers. All sperks. Couldn't go it in paint. Limits of the art. Limits of everything. Limits of my fingers which are all swole up at the joints. No fingers, no swell, so swell, no art, Old Renoir painting his red girls with the brushes strapped to wrists. Best things he ever did. Monuments. (p. 27)

When Coker reminds Jimson of the bus expenses she had to spend for him the other day, the artist is lost in his own world. He is trying to put into the Eve of his painting the natural innocence of Sara whom he had met some time age :

> Yes, I thought, alivoh, Eve should be a woman of forty with five childeen and grey hairs coming, trying on a new velvet. Looking at herself in the glass, as if she'd never seen herself before. And the children fighting round the dustbin in the yard. And Adam smoking his pipe in the local. And telling lies about his spring onions. Works of passion and imagination. (p. 42)

Jimson has faith in deeper insights, imaginative thrusts, creative upsurges and flashes of vision. There is a remarkable scene in the novel where, while Coker and the businessman Hickson haggle over the price of Jimson's paintings, the artist affirms that salvation lies in creation :

> But what you get on the inside, I said to myself, is the works --it's SOMETHING THAT GOES ON GOING ON. Hold on to that, old boy, I said, for it's the facts of life. It's the ginger in the giner bread. It's the apple in the dumpling. It's the jump in the OLD MOSQUITO. It's the kick in the old horse. It's the creation. And that's where it's leading me. Right up to that blasted picture of mine. (p. 104)

Thinking on the Fall he considered its universality in time, combining in metaphysical imagination, the ordinary and the sublime :

> ...what happends to a thousand Eves and Adams every night of the week somewhere under the willows or the palm tree shade—it's a long way from a tea-party. It's not pleasure, or peace, or contemplation, or comfort, or happiness—it's a Fall. Into the pit. The ground gives way, and down you go, head over heels. Unless, of course, you know how to fly. To rise again on your wings. (p. 104)

The most appealing aspect of Jimson's personality is his positive commitment to art. John Laird, stressing this free moral choice in every conscious individual, writes :

> The deed is *his*, we are told, precisely in so far as *he* is its author and in effective control. There may be a sense in which a worm is the author of some of its wriggles. In a man what is fundamental is the type of self-government. This in its turn is self-determination by knowledgeable choke, the knowledge in question involving both a serviceable knowledge of the agent's own powers, and the understanding of good and of right. *His* actions spring from *his* knowledgeable decisions, from the decisions which he makes when in his right mind.[30]

Jimson has made a choice and has decided to keep himself absorbed in his chosen profession. He knows that idleness saps his creative energies. Just out of hospital where he had been admitted after being beaten on a swindling charge and still convalescing in Coker's hut, he is tired of his lazy life and impatient to proceed with his next work that will be a masterpiece of his life :

> Even one day in bed was putting a cramp on my ideas, tucking them up in a tight parcel. My imagination was working inwards instead of outwards : it was fitting things into a

30. John Laird, *On Human Freedom* (London, 1947), p. 54.

> pattern, instead of letting them grow together. If I stayed in the boat-shed for a week under Cokey, I said, I could say good-bye to my creation—it would turn into a little square picture with four corners and a middle. However big I made it on the wall, it would be a piece of art work. A put-up job. A jigsaw of the back room. Whereas a real picture is a flowers, a geyser, a fountain, it hasn't got a pattern but a Form. It hasn't got corners and middle but an Essential Being. And this picture of mine, the Creation, had to be a creation. A large event. And no one can feel largely except in the open air. (p. 240)

Jimson is engaged on The Creation, the biggest and the greatest painting of his life on the wall of an old church building, while the policemen on the instructions of the local councillors start demolishing the building as unsafe. Jimson, unperturbed, gets on with his job with full gusto and ultimately the dream of his life materializes. Unbounded is his joy to see the painting successfully completed :

> And just then the whale smiled. Her eyes grew bigger and brighter and she bent slowly forward as if she wanted to kiss me. I had a shock. I was touched, of course, to see this affection in a favourite child, but I thought I must be dreaming again. "My dear girl", I said, "my petsie—do be careful—remember your delicate constitution". (p. 295)

Immediately after this, the building comes crashing down to the ground as an anti-climax to the magnificence of the scene just described :

> And all at once the smile in half, the eyes crumpled, and the whole wall fell slowly away from my brush ; there was a noise like a thousand sacks of coal falling down the Monument, and then nothing but dust ; a regular fog of it. I couldn't believe it, and no doubt I was looking a little surprised with my brush in my hand, and my mouth open, because when the dust began to clear I saw through the cloud about ten thousand angles in caps, helmets, bowlers and even one top hat, sitting on walls, dustbins, gutters,

> roofs, window sills and other people's cabbages, laughing. That is funny, I thought, they've all seen the same joke. God bless them. It must be a work of eternity, a chestnut, a horse-laugh. (p. 295)

Jimson has had a fall and suffers several bone fractures, but he retains his sense of human when he tries to pacify the angry Nosy, calling the whole occurrence as 'a resolute act of anti-aggression'. (p. 296)

Jimson is defeated in the same way as, Cary has written, 'many young rebels, young geniuses are defeated.[31] But Jimson is not going to turn his back on the profession and while he is being taken to hospital, he still hopes to have a new studio and paint new things. He has a religious passion for his painting, in spite of his comic freaks. Art is his psychological nourishment in an atmosphere of social tension. Gulley Jimson is at times rowdy, dishonest and outrageous but, nonetheless, a visionary obsessed artist. He rises in the social scale because of his enlightened consciousness that his profession should be followed through all vicissitudes of life and even under discouraging conditions. Gulley Jimson is a modern hero. Wayne C. Booth, making a distinction between the Victorian hero and the modern hero, writes :

> The Victorian hero after enough won our sympathies because his heart was in the right place. Many modern heroes win our allegiance because their aesthetic sensibilities will not be denied, or because they live life to the hilt, or simply because they are victims of their surroundings.[32] Jimson has refreshing inner toughness that inspires confidence in the cause which he pursues with messianic zeal. A life devoid of creative activity is unthinkable to him. The most appealing aspect of Jimson's character is, according to Car-

31. Joyce Cary, *Art and Reality*, p. 93.
32. Wayne C. Booth, *The Rhetoric of Fiction* (Chicago, 1961), p. 132.

lyle King, 'to be really alive ..in a state of continuous creation'.[33] Jimson's character illustrates the major paradox of Cary. The creator is symbolically destroyed by his own creation, although he finds himself lifted out of the world of material values into the realm of his own visions. That constitutes the human reality in this novel.

The Horse's Mouth is a comic tour de force. Potts in his book *Comedy* makes a distinction between tragedy and comedy and defines'tragedy' as an expression of the natural pride of man, defending himself as a sentiment being with a will and convictions of his own against all the forces, human and superhuman, and human, that fight against him; and comedy as an expression of the natural modesty of man, mixing with his kind, and defending them and himself against megalomania, egoism, misanthropy, and the other forces of disintegration inside human nature'.[34]. Jimson is no egoist. Although he has no money to buy material for his paintings, he is not spiteful against the capitalists who, he believes, might help in the promotion of original art. He tells his friend Walter in a conversation :

"So you're for the millionaries".

"The more the better, Walter. In my view, everybody ought to be millionaries". (p. 245). We cannot dub Gulley as good or bad for 'in comedy character consists not so much in goodness or wickedness as in efficiency or inefficiency : in courage or cowardice, cleverness or stupidity, good sense or folly'.[35]

Cary threw a veil of comedy over Jimson's constant preoccupation with his paintings. It is quite obvious that the need for comic paraphernalia arose to externalise Jimson's conflict between his urge for expression and his social predicament, since comedy, unlike tragedy, does not deal with human nature against a comic background. This distinction is incisively made by Potts :

---

33. Carlyle King, "Joyce Cary and the Creative Imagination", *Tamarack Review* (No. 10, Winter, 1959), p. 43.
34. L.J. Potts, *Comedy* (London, 1948), p. 114.
35. *Ibid.*, p. 124.

> Tragedy is a bulward of human self-respect against the superhuman or inhuman forces pressing upon us from all sides. Comedy is our corresponding weapon against the forces of disintegration within human society, and against the germs of anarchy and defeatism in our own minds.[36]

One cannot mistake the series of Jimson's intriguing tricks for his real self which is essentially creative. Gulley's character, a complex of seriousness and frivolity, is the reflection of the confused values of the society he lives in. Here in lies the explanation for his eccentricity. All comic writers, according to Potts, 'must have a norm in view. To detect eccentricity, you must have a centre ; that is to say a consistence, if not consciously worked out, standard of character and conduct'.[37]

It is difficult to reconcile the claims of Jimson's artistic imagination expressed in a language reaching the heights of poetic excellence with his easy relapse into uncivilized conduct. But the significance of the comic structure of the novel lies in the fact that it brings to light 'the resourcefulness and pugnacity of a little man willing to take on all comers.[38] The last words of the bruised and broken Gulley to the run is for the risible :

> "How don't you enjoy life, mother. I should laugh all round my neck at this minute if my shirt wasn't a bit on the tight side". "It would be better for you to pray". "Same thing, mother". (p. 297)

The three novels, *Herself Surprised, To Be a Pilgrim* and *The Horse's Mouth*, are remarkable creations. They deal with the chaos of human life and within it reveal reality or The Ultimate. In *Herself Surprised* the reality emerges through an

36. *Ibid.*, p. 44.
37. *Ibid.*, p. 47.
38. Kenneth Hamilton, "Boon or Thorn ? Joyce Cary and Samuel Beckett on Human Life", *The Dalhousie Review*, xxxviii (Winter, 1959), p. 435.

individual consciousness, in *To Be a Pilgrim* through a household community and in *The Horse's Mouth* through an isolated artist, sunk in life yet risen to a vision. The novels flow in turgid waters from life to a pool of light or LIFE. They are great stories of human reality.

CHAPTER V

Dogmatic Reality

The approach to fiction, in special cases, can be through dogma, one of the frontiers of knowledge which can be legitimate even as philosophy is to poetry as stated by T.S. Eliot in *The Sacred Wood.* Dogma or dogmatic reality can appear in two forms in a novel. First, the story can be written under the directing impulse of one dramatic idea or the sanction of a faith as in Cardinal Newman's novel *Loss and Gain* or the fictionalized autobiography of his own conversion through the character of Charles Reding. He passes through doubt and distress and eventually makes his choice of becoming a Roman Catholic. The climax occurs in the dialogue between Father Aloysius and Charles Reding :

> "You, dear Reding", said Father Aloysius, "have keen fresh feelings ; mine are blunted by familiarity".
>
> "No Willis", he made answer, "you have taken the better part be times, while I have loitered. Too late have I known Thee, O Thou ancient Truth, too late I found thee, First and only Fair".[1]

The second way dogmatic reality can appear in a novel is is by the complete transmutation of beliefs in the wider framework of humanism. It is not religion but the religions which concern them. This is the research of U.C. Knoepffmacher in his book *Religious Humanism and the Victorian Novel* (1965). George Eliot, Walter Pater and Samuel Butler were preoccupied with the aesthetic and not the doctrinal view of religion :

---

1. John Henry Newman, *Loss and Gain* (London, 1876), p. 431.

> These three novelists shared a large measure of experience, response and hope. All were anti-rationalistic and anti-doctrinal—relativism of truth.[2]

In Joyce Cary we have both the relativism of truth as well as the absolutism of truth or the influence of religion on human character. These are given through the fixity of purpose in and the changeableness of life as shown in the second trilogy *Prisoner of Grace* (1952), *Except the Lord* (1953) and *Not Honour More* (1955).

Prisoner of Grace (1952) depicts the political life of Chester Nimmo. To avoid the misreading of a political novel Cary warns that politics is more than just narrowness or a profession, it includes the whole of life :

> The difficult of a book about a politician is that people will tend to read it as a book about government. But politics is the art of human relations, an aspect of all life.[3]

The narrator of the novel is Nina, the wife of Nimmo. Cary writes about the point of view in the novel :

> I wanted to tell the story through the eyes of a wife whose marriage needs a great deal of management. I wanted to give the complete political scene.[4]

She describes her childhood when, her parents having died of cholera in India, she became an orphan and was brought up by her aunt Miss Latter at Palm Cottage. She had a companion, Jim Latter, her cousin. They were found of each other in childhood and when they grew up they had confidential relations. Nina was seventeen when she came to know Chester Nimmo, then a clerk in a certain Bing's office. Aunt Letter and political connections. She was on several committees at

2. U.C. Knoepffmacher, *Religious Humanism and the Victorian Novel* (New Jersey, 1965), p. 18.
3. Joyce Cary, Prefatory Essay to *Prisoner of Grace*, Carfax Edition (London Reprinted 1960), p. 5.
4. *Ibid.*

Tarbiton and used to pull strings. Nimmo supplied her with information on local affairs. Nimmo was drawn to Nina and proposed to marry her. Nina, already betrothed to Jim, turned down the offer. He sought the help of Aunt Latter. She knew that Nina had inherited five thousand pounds ; she was shrewd enough to foresee that with Nina's money Nimmo could carve out a political career for himself. Eventually under her aunt's pressure. Nina married Nimmo. She did not love him. But Nimmo's triumph was to win her by his adroitness :

> Indeed, one of Chester's clevernesses was to take responsibility for everything. He even did my packing and unpacking for me, and (having the lightest and neatest fingers as well as being a man of tremendous energy) would act as my maid, and help me to dress and undress (but only to a point ; he was very respectful of my modesty), and even sew on my buttons and brush and comb my hair and plait it for the night. I had never been so coddled. He treated me like a princess, or rather as a princess is reported to be treated. (p. 26)

His love for Nina is true and he prays for a happy wedded life. Nina writes of it :

> It is true that in our religious ideas (if you can call mine religious) we did not agree. I had been a little startled on our first night together to hear him murmur (but we were both so nervous at the time that I was not sure if I had heard him properly or if he knew what he was saying) something like a prayer for God's blessing on our union, which seemed to me so comic at such a moment that I had almost laughed. But luckily I was so shy of him it was only afterwards I realised that he had really meant to pray and that what he had meant by our "union "was just what I had thought so unsuitable for prayer. I was, I think, even a little shocked. (pp. 26-7)

The divide in Chester's character was his fidelity to God and religion and his adventurism in politics.

There is a religious strain in Chester which is set forth by Nina in different parts of the novel. While honeymooning with Nina in Italy Chester hated the churches as they followed rituals which militated against his idea of religion as a communion between the human soul and God :

> He meant that they were full of saints and candles. For he had a horror of the Roman religion and said that wherever it had power you found ignorance and oppression and dirt and poverty. I said that perhaps that was because miserable ignorant people needed a nice rich artistic kind of religion, but this also shocked him and he said with his religiour voice "artistic religion isn't religion at all—how could it be ? There is only one true religion—between a man's soul and his God. (p. 28)

Chester was a supporter of popular education, but some christian fanatics opposed him on this issue. Consequently, he lost his nomination for radical membership in Chorlock. This did not depress dim. Rather he prayed to God for His blessing on this rival. He held a prayer meeting where he despised himself for being ambitious Nina comments :

> You must never forget that Chester was a truly religious man and always on his guard (perhaps because of his special temptations) against a low idea of human nature and mean worldly ambitions. (p. 67)

Till such time as a clerk in Bing's office, Chester manages to get elected to the Tarbiton Municipal Council, which is the beginning of his political career. Succcess flares up Nimmo's ambition to such an extent that he cannot rest content with council membership, becomes a demagogue, manipulate people to vote him into parliament and ultimately becomes a minister in the government. The innocent Nina, happy within the percints of family life, is dragged into public life to play politics for the success of her husband. Nina's description of the political atmosphere in which truth and falsehood are dangerously mixed reveals the depth of her confusion :

> I don't say that they said openly what a good thing it was for them to provoke violence and get people killed. In fact I don't believe for a moment that they even thought it. It was at this time I began to feel among "political" people the strange and horrible feeling which afterwards became so familiar to me (but not less horrible), of living in a world without any solid objects at all, of floating day and night through clouds of words and schemes and hopes and ambitious and calculations where you could not say that this idea was obviously selfish and dangerous and that one quite false and wicked because all of them were relative to something else. The lies were mixed up with some truth (like Chester's belief in a class plot), and the selfish calculations (like Goold's Planning to make trouble at Lilmouth) melted at the edges into all kinds of "noble" ideals (like Chester's passion for freedom and free speach). (pp. 59-60)

Chester Nimmo sacrifices principle for self-interest. At first he pledges himself with sincereity to the uplift of the masses, the landless and the illiterate. Gradually, whenever his political position is at stake, he upholds a principle and capitalizes on a burning issue to his own advantage. An example of his opportunism is seen at the time of the first world war. Before the war, feeling the pulse of the British people that they hate war, Nimmo becomes an avowed pacifist and gains in popularity. The war breaks out and a shake-up in the British government is imminent. The old government is replaced by an emergency war-cabinet. While people are looking forward to his resignation as a protest against the war policy of the govenment. Nimmo, fearing and end to his political career, forget the pledge and joins the war-cabinet. Later, his statement full of polemics, explaining the need for a change of decision, takes in the simple-minded and even Nina :

> I was quite moved by his words—they made me feel (like thousands of his supporters who had been raging against him) short-sighted and narrow-minded, lacking in "vision".

> And I told myself that Chester had relly been surprised by the sudden attack on Belgium, that he had been indispensable in the war cabinet, that it had been his duty, just as he had said, to ignore a pledge given under other circumstances ; in fact, that in real life one cannot always keep pledges.
>
> And this is quite true. No one on earth can prove that Chester was not doing a rather noble act (risking his very honour) when he "ratted" on his pledges. Quite possibly (if he had time, in thd middle of such important and urgent "public responsibilities", to consider the point at all) he believed it himself, even at the time. He certainly came to believe it afterwards. (p. 268)

Nimmo becomes an unprincipled politician and crushes his conscience. He suffers a moral collapse of the kind deprecated by Millard Spencer Everett in his book *Ideals of Life* :

> A truly moral person is one who will stand up for his principles no matter how much he may have to suffer and no matter how much disapproval he incurs.[5]

Chester, as he rises in political stature, thinks more of ideas than palpable human relations. Nina describes how he becomes identified with an abstract concept like the government and is out off from the public contract. His greed for money increases as he thinks more of his personal security :

> A man so burdened as a War Minister has to be surrounded by a wall of routine—he is like an institution which would not work at all unless it was organised. But it meant that visitors had often to be kept amused for hours, and our expenses, especially for liquor shot up to amazing heights. It was a mercy that Chester's shares had begun, in in the second year of war, to go up with them. As I discovered, a great man, or at least a stateman in power, had

5. Millard Spencer Everett, *Ideals of Life* (New York, 1954), pp. 538-9.

> to be rich ; and though the Government gives a Prime Minister all that is necessary in housing and servants, we had nothing from it except the bare pay and a policeman to keep anarchists or Irishmen from murdering us in our beds. (p. 270)

For Chester the human soul is subordinated to the machinery that is government. This is in reversal to what C.E.M. Joad writes in his book *Guide to the Philosophy of Morals and Politics* :

> I have my doubts about the immortality, but I have none about the importance, of individuals. Souls are souls even if their life here is transitory. and though they may not be immortal, it is none the less, I conceive, the business of government to treat them as if they were.[6]

The relations between Nimmo and his wife were often strained. There was no union of hearts between them. Nina felt his oppressive presence. Once after a quarrel Nina writes in the sharpness of a smile :

> To quarrel with Chester, to deal with him at all, was like struggling with a shark whose teeth all point the same way. His love and his anger both swallowed me down a little further into a horrible stuffy darkness. (p. 175)

She resents her husband's cold calculations in love. When Nimmo divorces her after thirty years of married life, she turns to her lover Jim and marries him. The next blow to Nimmo is his defeat in the post-war elections. Editor Round's scathing commentary on the character of Nimmo might echo Cary's own moral judgment on this wily politician :

> We need not waste pity on the fate of Lord Nimmo. I say with all due respect of my words that this man, so easily corrupted—this evil man—was one of the chief architects of our destruction. Not content with selling his perso-

6. C.E.M. Joad, *Guide to the Philosophy of Morals and Politics* (London, 1938), p. 13.

nal honour for power and cash, he left nothing undone to destory the very soul of our great cause. And we see the consequences to-day in the final divorce of politics and morality—the universal collapse of christian values—materialism rampant and unashamed—the naked persuit of gain by all conditions of men—the philosophy grap which dominates all programmes. (p. 262)

Finally pushed out of his political world full of manoeuvrings and with its human relations measured in terms of immediate utility rather than abiding ties, Nimmo decides to write a memoir of his past life, visits Palm Cottage, the residence of Jim and Nina who is no longer his wife and seeks her assistance. There he shows his further degradation and perversion. The same Chester who, while a boy, had shied away fram prostitutes, received exhortations on universal brotherhood and considered marriage as the union of two souls, makes a criminal assault on Nina like a lustful beast at an age when he is expected to be emotionally mature and self-restrained.

Chester's life is full of contradictions in the novel. He is married to Nina who belongs to an upper class family but he is vehemently opposed to her class : 'You don't know what class is, you don't know how different you are. Why, you would have more in common with a negre—I mean a negro gentleman—than with Bill Code'. (p. 33). But he wants Nina to be richly dressed and cultivate aristocratic grace for his success. While Nina's social position is the key to his rise, he is bent upon abolishing the landed gentry to which she belongs. Later, he changes his stand. Always an impassioned critic of the landlords, he is not only ready to become one himself but is anxious to make his son Tom a hereditary squire : 'Chester admitted quite freely that the old landed families were a valuable factor of stability and that squires like the squire of Buckfield, with energy and capital, should play an important part in the national life'. (p. 313). Nimmo's religious views too are incompatible with his political trickery. He confuses religion with politics as Nina writes : 'Chester's feelings and energies seemed to run into each other ; his religion stirred up his politics and his politics stirred up his religion, and both of them stirred up his affections and his imagination and his imagination kept everything else in a perpetual turmoil'. (p. 395). Chester is, no doubt, a 'composite of the opposites'.[7] Giles Mitchell in a research paper in *Modern Fiction* Studies writes :

> ...his inner springs of action are basically anarchic. In seeking mass good, he ignores the moral prerogatives of the *Consensus gentium*. His work is primarily ego oriented, and it becomes progressively more so throughout his life. The subtle tension between the demands of common good and personal ambition he is never able to reconcile.[8]

He swings between principle and expediency.

Nina's character, too, is a rich portrayal of moral ambiguities, although Elizabeth Kerr believes that she is 'incapable of self-deception'.[9]

Nina, in spite of her knowledge that Nimmo is cunning holds herself responsible for all acts of omission and commission done during her association with him. That moral confusion has already plagued her is clear from her own confession : 'I think I was probably capable of anything because I had begun to suspect that I could reconcile myself to anything'. (pp. 24-5). She further writes : 'It seemed that I was two women, one of them quite furious still and watchful of every move of this cunning enemy, and one of them so close and sympathetic to him that she felt all his feelings like her own'. (p. 44). Nina's conflicting loyalities—her love for him and her duty towards Chester—form the recurring pattern in the structure of the novel. She oscillates between submission towards, and animo-

---

7. Frederick R. Karl, *A Reader's Guide to the Contemporary English Novel* (London, 1963), p. 136.
8. Giles Mitchell, "Joyce Cary's *Prisoner of Grace*", *Modern Fiction Studies*, IX, Nos 3 (Autumn, 1963), p. 275.
9. Elizabeth Kerr, "Joyce Cary's Second Trilogy", *University of Toronto Quarterly*. XXIX (April, 1960), p. 318.

sity against, Nimmo and finds herself in a perpetual dilemma in the course of events and critical situations that she passes through. Andrew Wright's comment on Nina's character is pertinent :

> So the formal device of the book clearly emphasizes the personal boundaries of Nina's life. She stands between the two men sometimes as mediator, but always a comforter to them both.[10]

She repeatedly attempts to leave Nimmo for Jim's sake, but the reader is dazed to see at the end that Nina is unmindful not only of Nimmo's presence in Palm Cottage but of his criminal assults on her in spite of the fact that she is no longer his wife. The reader fails to understand when Nina cannot drive him out in spite of her can did admission that she had a peaceful life after her divorce from Nimmo. It is clear that she has no feeling for Nimmo at all. She is no longer under his charms, but she thinks that she is attached to Chester by a 'marriage of thirty years that was all the more a "part of me", because (she) had suffered in it'. (p. 400). To drive him out was like committing 'a mean crime against something bigger than love'. (p. 402). In the end, after a life torn between love and hatred, she still has the same equivocal attitude :

> And I knew then that I should never get rid of Chester, that I dared not do so. And I saw that it was no good pretending that I merely tolerated an old man's whims because he was pitiful—I did not love Chester and I had never loved him, but now, more than ever, at the end of his life, I was in his power. (p. 400)

Nina, therefore, is not capable of balanced thinking and her moral uncertainty comes out in her relationship with Nimmo. She continues to consider Nimmo great while the prima facie evidence of Nimmo's degradation is already established and substantiated by her own statement. Elizabeth R. Bettman points out Nina's weakness as 'an absence of moral commit-

---

10. Andrew Wright, *op. cit.*, p. 139.

ment'.[11] Nina calls herself 'a women who excused everyone and everything because I did not want the trouble of condemning...' (p. 277). This statement calls into question Nina's professed intention to vindicate the greatness of Nimmo at the very beginning of the novel :

> I am writing this book because I understand that "revelations" are soon to appear about that great man who was once my husband, attacking his character, and my own. And I am affraid that they will be believed simply because now-a-days everyone believes the worst of a famous man. The greater his name, the worse the stories. (p. 9)

That she completely falls to pass verdict on Nimmo's deeds which she finds distasteful on several occasions reinforces the point of a moral ambivalence in Nina's character. But Cary has an explanation for this in the preface :

> The book was called *Prisoner of Grace* because Nina was hold to her husband by her sense that he was on the whole a good man. She recoiled from destroying his career because she felt that he was trying to do right. It has been objected that she was not a prisoner of grace in any true sense, because her motive was selfish, she was afraid to spoil her happiness by a crime. But, after all, this means that she is the kind of person who is afraid of guilt, and such people are not in fact bad people.[12]

The antinomy is Between Chester's religion and his politics. He dictates to Bootham on the young :

> What has happened to you all ? Why do you leave your souls to die by the way side ? (p. 393)

It is chester who is a should by the wayside. The "moral relativism" in which he is plunged makes him a tragic figure. Nina was a prisoner of grace of she was within the influence of

11. Elizabeth R. Bettman, "Joyce Cary and the Problem of Political Morality", *Antioch Review*, XVII (Summer, 1957), p. 269.
12. Joyce Cary, Prefatory Essay to *Prisoner of Grace*, p. 6.

the "real Chester", the man with a faith who gradually broke away from it and the church from which he stayed away. It was fear that kept Nina in his control. She was terrified by Chester's hell fire :

> I should despise myself, which is, I suppose, what Chester means when he says that such and such a "poor devil" is "demned". And I am terrified of 'damnation", for it would destory my happiness and all the joy of my life, and Jim can only shoot me dead. (p. 402)

It is a broken prism of dogmatic reality that we can get in the two character, Nina and Chester. The influence of religion on their souls is differently shown and poses certain problems. Cary discussing Nina's character writes :

> Another question was, how could Nina, with her very slender grasp of religion, be described as subject to grace ?[13]

Cary answers it himself 'grace is not a rare and strange from the mysterious depths of things ...it is an influence as common as the weather and persistent as the heart muscle'.[14] Chester, in antithesis to Nina, also poses a question 'how does a real politician, the handler, the manager of people, who is also a man of principle, keep his principles ?'[15] The answer to this question on Chester is that in politics he was always "in the middle of a violent storm", he was never "in harbour" (p. 230) ; in religion he had glimpses of truths intermittently grasped like flickering gleams from a distant lighthouse.

A Prisoner of Grace deals with the relativism of dogmatic reality in 'the over-changing complexities of human affairs', the next novel *Except the Lord* exemplifies the absolutism of dogmatic reality. The beliefs expressed in the lives of the characters have behind them the sanctions of religion, not the doctri-

13. *Ibid.*, p. 7.

14. *Ibid.*

15. *Ibid.*, p. 5.

nes of a private would but of 'the world outside the mind'[16] or an objective reality as stated in the Bible, in the prayers and hymns of the christian church. These are the 'permanent and highly obstinate facts' against which Cary sets 'permanent and highly obstinate human nature'.[17]

Except the Lord (1953) is a memoir of Chester Nimmo composed by him at Palm Cottage. He is old and recalls his boyhood and youth from 1854 the date of his birth to 1879 when he was twenty five years old with nostalgic reminiscence and even with a sense of guilt as he fell away from the beautiful and the innocent. The novel is what Chester says 'a drama of my soul'. (p. 160)

The Nimmo family in *Except the Lord* is deeply Evangelical, sincerely devoted to God. The father of Chester Nimmo is a farmer at High-fallow in Devonshire. He was a 'religious man, of profound faith and strong conviction. It would be a great error to set him down as narrow or bigoted'. (p. 57). Nimmo's mother is an embodiment of goodness, purity and piety, free from all taints of selfish motives. Nimmo's description of his mother is one of spontaneous reverence :

> For all her gaiety, her humour, my mother was a dedicated creature. Her life was inward and she trembled before a god that judged the very heart. When I kneeled in her lap and whispered my first prayers into her breast, I cannot tell what ideas that bed time ceremoney stirred in my infant mind. But was I wrong to feel that I knelt in a holy place and communicated with a spirit which was then in all its gentle and modest service truly one with the most High 7. (p. 11)

The children of this family have been taught to keep away from lies and falsehood and to profess nothing but the truth, the only way to win the grace of God. This teaching is so

16. John Teeling, "Joyce Cary's Moral World", *Modern Fiction Studies*, IX, No. 3 (Autumn, 1963), p. 277.
17. Joyce Cary, *Art and Reality*, p. 19.

embeded in their consciousness that Nimmo, having once committed a mistake, is overwhelmed with guilt and the dread of consequences as in the Old Testament :

> My only memory of grief at High fallow comes from quite another source. I had committed some fault, and told a lie about it and not been discovered. And I had been taught that bad children who do not confess and repent will go to hell.
>
> I do not remember anything but the terror-possibly for a very short time before I was found out, and punished, and so absolved. The fear of hell, the punishment of sin, how the modern parent revolts from such teaching. Yet I will assert that far from doing us children harm, it was a sure foundation to the world of four confidence, a master girder in our palace of delight. For we saw its justice, we knew, in the common phrase, exactly where we were—the wicked would be punished, and the good should have reward. (pp. 8-9)

Religion, for the Nimmo family, was not just a vague assumption that God exists, but it was bound up with the Nonconformist church.

Once Georgina, Nimmo's sister, had a collision with the Battwell girl in Shagbrook. It was an accident and the gril feels sorry for this. But Georgina has already lost her temper and blinded by an impulse of aggression she beats the girl severaly. The matter is reported to her father who is stunned by his daughter's wickedness. He makes her pray and repent, because he knows that prayer has a redeeming effect. The seriousness and the assured confidence of the father in repentance and the dramatic transition in Georgina from wild hysterics to calm composure are described :

> My father looked at her for some time with a perplexed air, and asked her then if she did not think she ought to be beaten when she was so wicked and so sullen when she did not answer, he shook his head and said, 'Ah, my poor

Georgy. So that old devil is back within 'ee after all our prayers—and worse than ever'.

And when Georgina remained silent, locked in her pride, he signed and said that still he knew how she had tried to fight that devil and so he could not find it in his heart to beat her. In the name of Jesus who had put grace into her heart before when she was at her wickedest, he would pray again for her poor soul. So let her kneel down with him and they would pray together...

...To him the battle in Georgina's heart between the devils of her temper and her passions, and the grace of God's love, was as real as any fight upon a fair-day.

Georgina stood still and unrelenting, but the nervous shake in her arms had now communicated itself to her body, she was quivering all over like a plucked string, and my father said, 'Ah Sam, see how it shakes the poor little maid, her souldis all torn with the fight'. And he drew her aside and knelt down on some sacks next the wall, and suddenly before he could speak, Georgina gave a cry and threw herself down on the ground and caught him round the ankles. She was weeping so violently that her body seemed to jump on the stones. (p. 34)

The most shocking crisis in the family is the death of the good and angelic mother, Mrs. Nimmo, who had been stricken with consumption. Grim poverty deprived her of the rich nutritive diet and a climatic change in some foreign country that the patient of such a disease badly needed. The children are deeply distressed and upset over their mother's death. Georgina, the eldest among the children, breaks down in sorrow and says bitterly that her mother would have survived if she had been sent off to France and provided with plenty of wine and fruits. Nimmo's father is no less shocked and disturbed but he maintains his equanimity with remarkable courage. His reply to Georgina in a restrained voice is a glowing testimony to his unfaltering trust in God :

> It is not for us to question the work of Providence, the Lords given and He takes away. You did not earn yourself. George, and you would have no right to cry if you were crooked. (p. 39)

Proof of his deep-rooted attachment to the good wife is the lavish expense he incurred on his wife's funeral rites, a tribute before the world in honour of a great women, Chester recollects :

> I had not asked myself then why throughout all the world, a family may still spend all they have, and more, on the funeral of a parent, wife or husband ; I had not asked myself, in short, why mankind, even the humblest, set certain responsibilities of the soul, certain duties of the heart, above expense, even when that expense may bring they years of real want—and why, too, those who know to honour goodness and truth in their hearts feel it laid upon them to make those reverent feelings known.
>
> I have never known a man less inclined to ostentation than my father. He was, anything, as we shall see, too indifferent to the opinions of others, too independent in his living. The sum he spent, largely on credit, on my mother's funeral was not only His statement before the world that my mother was worthy of honour, but also, in the mysterious domain of our spiritual life, an act of gratitude and worship towards the dead. And how better to measure that gratitude than by a personal sacrifice. (p. 43)

Religion to Nimmo's father is the sheet-anchor of life and not just a sheer upsurge of subjective feeling as besets modern life at the present time :

> In the spiritual life of to-day, then, religious experience is to a great degree in bad repute ; and this is because it is quite wrongly restricted to "feeling", its value being then estimated according to the intensity of such feeling.[18]

18. G. Van Der Leeuw, *Religion in Essence and Manifestation*, tr. J.E. Turner (London, 1938), pp. 460-61.

In *Except the Lord* there is a correspondence between feeling and action as the children look upon their father as the embodiment of Truth and a God like presence :

> My father had never lost his temper with us, never beaten us, but we had for him that feeling often described as fear which is something quite different and far deeper them alarm. It was that sense which, without irreverence, I have thought to find expressed by the great evangelists when they speak of the fear of God. One does not fear God because he is terrible, but because he is literally the soul of goodness and truth, because to do him wrong is to do wrong to some mysterious part of oneself, and one does not know exactly what the consequence may be. (p. 49)

Nimmo's father would prefer starvation to money dishonourably earned. His Protestantism gave him an exalted sense of personal dignity.[19] When Georgina is employed at a bar in order to support the family, he upbraids his daughter. He is against drink :

> ...he would say of drink that no doubt it did no harm to those who could control their appetites, but it was the duty of christians to consider their weaker brethern and to forgo a slight and transient pleasure for a great and lasting good. And the good should be to their own salvation too, in the discipline of their flesh. (p. 58)

Nimmo's father was a theist who lived like a saint in exalted contemplation. This is seen in his attitude in the miners' strike at Ranstove, because of the refusal of poorer mines to

---

19. It is, therefore, not possible to agree with Hersehel Baker who in his book *The Dignity of Man* charges Protestant Religion with having dispensed with individual dignity :

> 'Protestant theology denied man's claims to the dignity based on rational conduct, it enable him to find a new dignity in the economic exploitation of his environment.

> Herschel Baker, *The Dignity of Man* (Harvard University Press, 1947), p. 332.

pay the workers because of the big slump in the tine prices. He He plunges into vigorous relief work. He becomes treasurer of the friendly society, collects funds and appeals for the immediate starting of free soup kitchens to keep the strikers and their families alive. The children are surprised at their father's lack of discrimination between those who work more and those who work very little. But to a believer in God the Creater all men, whatever their rank abilities and strength, are equal :

> As for gratitude to those who served him, did he not thank God every night, in our own presence, for his children, sent to him for his comfort and blessing. True, he did not much distinguish between us as blessings—his own life was so entirely given to others without regard for return that he hardly noticed the difference between the labourer who, like Georgina, worked all through the day, and those like us who came in at the end of it and did comparatively little. He had that blindness to common justice between man and man which is not unusual among saints, who see all men as sunk so deep in obligation to God that their various merits are as corn to the height of the sky. One read shaking in the wind may be some inches tailler than another, but what are inches in the abyss of the eternal contemplation 7. (pp. 74-5)

This is the kind of transcendentalism that absolute religion gives, religion which 'cuts across and shatters the world of claims and counter claims, and thinks of the individual as "real" not in virtue of his finite nature but only in virtue of his spiritual membership of whole with which he identifies himself in thought and action. His standard of action, from the point of view of religion, is that he should act as an "expression" of the whole for the sake of the life of the whole'.[20]

Cary suggests that religious faith is beyond rational analysis and is just beliefs skin to what G. Van Der Leeuw describes :

20. W.D. Lamont, *The Principles of Moral Judgment* (Oxford, 1946), p. 163.

'To speak of faith is to speak of *truth*, in the sense not of correctness but of the authentic, valid, ultimate, conclusive and complete. And we observe immediately that we cannot speak about this truth, cannot say anything at all about it, until we have been seized by it, until we believe it : I have believed and therefore I speak'.[21] Nimmo's father, who believes in the Second Coming of Christ, fixes up a date, April 15, 1868 (p. 113), and a place called Black Man Tor for the same. On the day there is a huge turn out including a large number of learned people whose presence proves that faith is far stronger and more appealing than conceptual education. Nimmo's commentary on the scepticism of the so-called wise sounds like Cary's :

> I do not wonder that learned men shared my father's wild hope. What logic will answer the voice that murmurs in the brain night and day, 'There is no truth and goodness is a lie—love a trick'. What learning will cure the despair that rages in the flesh like cancer, eating a man alive.
>
> The marvel is that millions deny all hope and boast themselves wise. Men who for some reason for fear or vanity to take care to ask no questions that cannot be answered with a slide rule, who learn nothing, state nothing, but numbers, who, carefully withdrawing their dignity from the arena where men struggle and suffer so foolishly, take their padded seats in the stalls and raise critical eyebrows at the circus which is the agony of the world. (p. 117)

Somehow the prediction about the Doomsday and Christ's Resurrection does not come true. This comes as a shock to Chester Nimmo, now fourteen, and his brother Richard. For the first time his faith in God falters and he cases to have the same respect for his father as he used to have before with all the intensity of his natural feeling. We have a peep into his mind swinging between faith and scepticism as to the very existence of God and his attitude towards his father :

21. G. Van Der Leeuw, *op. cit.*, p. 535.

The faith that grows from childhood into the very texture of mind and soul can give it strength and unity which nothing earthly can destory. It has stood the utmost cruelty that man can invent, it is like the elastic steel of those tall houses which in an earthquake away each way but will not fall.

But if the steel be flawed and the frame of that house break, it cannot be mended, the sharp ends tear at the fabric till the whole is one wound. Better for that house if it had been built of cob, a low thing that neither dares the gale nor fears to be thrown down, a little mud will make it as good or bad as before.

I had been taught to believe but the frame of my faith had been broken—at the critical age of puberty, when above all a young needs confidence in his elders and leaders—when nature herself, as if to make up for that physical turmoil that she has injusted into his frame, has awakened in him also the power of devotion to a hero or a cause.

But I had no hero ; however my feelings, feelings implanted in me froi earliest childhood, recoiled from attheism, yet I could no longer respect my father. I saw him only as an ignorant man who had been deceived in a ridiculous manner and had made his family ridiculous. (p. 129)

There was an earlier wrench from his father than this in Nimmo's life, and that was when as a led he visited the Lilmouth Great Fair where he witnessed the play "Maria Marten". The theatre was a forbidden resort according to strict Evangelism. The play was about an innocent girl and a villain who murdered her. The emotional impact of this play on the boy Nimmo was tremendous for it gave him his first glimpse of evil :

Still stranger and more terrible truth, even in the midst of my horror at this monster in his blood guilt, I was aware of a fascinated admiration. When in his soliloquies at the front of the stage, his eyes, roving over the audinance, seemed to meet mine, they sent forth an indescribable

> thrill—it seemed that something flashed from the very centre of evil into my deepest soul. (pp. 93-4)

The power of evil and good were finally the theme of his unrevised sixteenth novel *The Captive and the Free.*

Bewildered, confused, conscious of his poverty and ignorance Chester Nimmo comes under the influence of Lanza, an Italian professor and refugee in Tarbiton, who believes in the Brotherhood of Man, Nimmo who has by now rejected all religious sermons is charmed to listen to the professor who speaks of 'love, that family love which guarded over all childhood, the love of fathers and mothers for their children, of brothers and sisters for each other'. (p. 135). Nimmo becomes a humanist and Lanza's speech 'appealed to experience, and an experience as deep and strong and true as it is universal. What man does not remember his mother's unselfish affection ? Who has not felt the impulsive goodness of a child ?' (p. 136). Some years later, he is co-opted by the Bethel chapel of Battwell on a certain charitable committee and his business is to report conditions in Battwell to Lord Slapton, the chief landlord. Later, in the Lord's absence, he is to report his duty to Miss Latter, Slapton's cousin, who becomes a shaping force in Nimmo's political career. Once during a visit to Palm Cottage, Miss Latter's residence, he is greeted by her niece Nina, small girl, whose innocence gives Nimmo an intuition into the essential goodness inherent in man :

> ...she was marked by unusual qualities of thoughtfulness and sincerity. That lucid and condid gaze which so powerfully affected the awkward and embarrassed young man was not only the revelation of childhood's natural innocence but of qualities unique in that child—an inborn truth—an essential generosity of affection which no cruelty of fate, no bitter experience of human perfidy, could ever tarnish. Faith hope—the profound charity which in the truest sense of the word rests in the love of God, and is indeed the very door of His grace—were innate in that spirit. (p. 140)

This sudden realization makes Nimmo see the folly of his

assumption that God and humanism are two different poles. He becomes convinced of the Divine spirit permeating the very rationale of humanism :

> I had rejected God and with God, the love, the charity, the assured faith in goodness that I had learnt in my own home. Now under another name, that of humanity. He was restored to his full grandeur and majesty as ruler of the world. For the miseries of that world were shown as the just and inevitable punishment of those who had turned their faces from that fundamental law of brotherhood. How should the world have joy which lived in joyless fear for its possessions ? (p. 141)

Nimmo's discovery that love for mankind is a manifestation of godliness or a divine quality finds further support in the following statement :

> The so-called "attributes" of God, too, are all comprehended within love. For these attributes are neither descriptions of God's uniqueness, nor edifying fantasies, nor even philosophic deductions, but experiences of the one love that is interpreted differently in each case. In love, again, the two demands, which we must address to religion, concur in being realized. That God is ultimate is expressed by the "attributes" of omnipotence ; but in each of these instances alike this is only a proclamation of the love that is experienced as ultimate.[22]

While serving on the Tarbiton Union Nimmo was beaten. He was in need of guidance. He went to London with his sister Georgina, met the markist Pring and with his help got a place in the Docker's union at Lilmouth. The dockers' strike was planned to subvert the ruling government and seize power. The strike having ended in a fiasco, Nimmo became a victim of conspiracy and suffered humiliation. In his disturbed state of mind after a break-away from faith he returns to it. His father prays quoting the beautiful text of Psalm 127, the first words of which furnish the title of this well written book :

22. G. Van Der Leeuw, *op. cit.*, p. 648.

Except the Lord build the house,
their labour is but lost that build it ;

Except the Lord keep the city,
the watchman waketh but in vain.

Lo, children and the fruit of the womb are an
heritage and gift that cometh of the Lord. (p. 284)

With dramatic suddenness self-realization dawns upon Nimmo. His remoir opens with these words :

> Yesterday, an old man nearing my end, I stood by the grave of a noble woman, one of the three noblest I have ever known, my mother, my sister, my wife. If I draw back now the curtain from my family life, sacred to memory, I do so only to honour the dead, and in the conviction that my story throws light upon the crisis that so fearfully shakes our whole civilization. It is the story of a crime, of a soul, my own, plucked back from the very edge of frustration and despair. (p. 5)

He is aware of his self-deception and bitterly critical of the world and evil :

> The world itself is young, we are but little removed from the time when writing was a wonder, when any written speech was magic. Words printed in books—Rousseau, Proudhon, Owne, Marx, what power they can weild. But it is the power of sorcerers—the spell they cast is abracadabra. And the fruit of their sorcery is egotism and madness, war and death.
>
> So evil is the brood of the slogans that the most spendid and noble battle cries, Liberty, Equality, Fraternity, bred nothing but new and more cunning, more hypocritical desports, better organized murger, popular nationalism drunk with the conceit of hooligans, militarism as the tool of demagogues, hatred not to be assuaged by the blood of millions and a century of tears. (p. 274)

Nimmo recalls the days when his father used to chant prayers with serene devotion and speak about the uniqueness of God with self-effecting humility. The psalm, still ringing in his ears, brings him an awareness of the greater need for a life of spiritual pursuits :

> And for me the music of that great psalm brought with it a thousand remembrances, my soul strieed and rose to it as to an old trumpet. And as the trumpet brings with it to the soldier more than he can speak or even analyse, vast regions of history, of his nation's glory, so I felt the release of a man who becomes for that moment greater than himself. I did not know then what had happened to me. I might say that it was years before I grasped the full significance of that prefoundest of truths not only for the man but for all his endeavours—not only in his family life but in his political activity—that unless he aim at the life of the soul then all his achievement will be a goal or a mad-house, self-hatred, corruption and despair. (p. 284)

The memory of Georgina, his sister who had the courage to look after the family selflessly after her mother's death when she was only twelve, and who worked so hard that she contracted consumption and died in the prime of her yough, overwhelms Nimmo with inexpressible gratitude to that extraordinary woman who made such a great, unimaginable sacrifice. Having forgotten to revisit the Shagbrook church where Georgina lies buried, in the forty years of his political life, Nimmo is repentant and rushes off to the grave to pay his homage to her. Standing by the grave mound, he has a mixed sensation of depression and elation. He realizes his own littleness and the futility of his pride, but the next moment he is reminded of his sister's insistence on devotion to one's duty and braces himself up for the task that lies ahead :

> Looking down on that mound in the furthest corner of Shagbrook churchyard, now no more than a geltel swelling of the turf, hidden under the long grass by the moor wall, I asked myself if it spoke more of pride or humbleness. For it said more plainly than Georgina had ever spoken

in life. No one knew my bitterness and I would not tell it. I wept in secret and learnt in the night of desolation. I made myself nothing and world was nothing to me.

The humbleness of a saint ? A boast so proud that no mogul could surpass it ? Or are they one in such devoted beings ?

Suddenly my blood quickened. I perceived that my memory of Georgina had failed and deceived me. It was here, in the vast silence of the moor, that her spirit lived, silently awaiting me whether I came or no. I had come at last and my heart was beating again strongly to a heart that could not know despair because it forgot itself in the duty of its love.

And my way was made plain. 'Here', I said, 'the story began and here it shall begin again, in the things I lived with this forgotten one, in the young cruelty of the world, in the making of four souls'. p. 287)

The novel is a triumph of moral absolutism, of dogmatic reality in Evangelical christianity. It deals with providence who plays His part in the 'mysterious domain of our spiritual life'. At the meeting of Dr. Leddra, the Baptist minister, the congregation sang :

O God our help in ages past
Our hope in years to come.

And Cary writes of the scene in the ecstatic prose and observation of Nimmo :

I have never forgotten that scene upon the combeside ; the sky above full of July sunlight, the stream glittering among the stones, a bird flying over and turning aside in alarm at the sight and sound of humanity in this quiet place, and the ragged crowd about the minister, men threatened with the ruin of their lives, raising their voices in chorus, hoarsely indeed, but with earnest apppeal in that hymn of prayer. (p. 68)

The book has many a paen to God, the centre of truth and reality, like this one of God's omnipresence :

> No doubt God is in all things. It is His life which maintains the physical world, as the soul of man carries his body for a vesture. But those who choose the mountains tops for that intuition of the numinous in us, in which it seems that we break through the boundaries of the word into the very centre of the Divine Mind, are not deceived. For the word and the works of man, however necessary to his worldly life, hide from his daily imagination the primitive grandeur of creation. (p. 118)

Faith in the reality of God's Being is most explicitly set forth here. This is not a rationalization of Cary's personal sentiment, but a fact which all religions accept. Wilmon Henry Sheldon in his book *God and Polarity* writes about the Divine Reality different from the phenomenal :

> Reality...is power, order, and value. Whatever is real maintains itself to some degree, is individual, itself and no other ; it has also character, ordered behaviour, is substance with attributes, specific powers.[23]

The last of the political trilogy is *Not Honour More* (1955). Cary had once written that his world is different from that of Henry James and that he strove to give the dramatic and a world in creation. Further : 'In this world, politics is like naviation in a sea without charts and wise men live the life of pilgrims'.[24] In *Not Honour More* we watch this sea in turmoil. What keeps the ship going is the compass of reality or that which never changes.

The narrator in this novel is Jim or as he is now, Captain James Latter, formerly District Officer in the Nigerian Political Service. He is Nina's husband after Nimmo divorced her. Nimmo is an old man in the fag end of his life. Nina too is

---

23. Wilmon Henry Sheldon, *God and Polarity* (New York, 1954), p. 123.
24. John Burrows and Alex Hamilton, "An Interview with Joyce Cary", *Paris Review*, VIII (Winter 1954-55) p. 71.

advanced in years after thirty years of terminated married life with Nimmo. The political setting is the labour strike of 1926 which sparked off a major crisis in the country. Nimmo finds the strike a good chance to steal the limelight. He 'wangles' himself into the Emergency Committee set to keep the peace. Contradictorily he excites the people and fans the revolution against injustice and corruption. He does this in a string speech at Shagbrook :

> "My friends make no doubt, as a freeman of England, I stand for revolution, the everlasting revolution. I am with you against the oppresssor whatever guise he wear. My friends, we meet today on ground sacred to the cause, I say the holy cause, of liberty, and sacred especially to my heart, at a moment most terribly fraught with destiny—yes, a day that will stand in history as a turning point, a crisis in the fate of the world. For you, my friends, Englishmen, freemen of the West, are entrusted with a fearful responsibilty, not only for the destiny of England, but of Europe, and the whole earth. Be in no doubt—you are the masters—power has passed to your hands. And your wrongs are deep and and perpetual, you would be perfectly justified if you used that power to tear the present scheme of things apart, to destory for ever a society which has turned a deaf ear to your legitimate complaint, and a blind eye from your gross and patient sufferings'. (pp. 106-7)

Nimmo is staying at Palm Cottage, the house of Nina and Jim. There he is having illicit relations with Nina who considers him the only man capable of hauling the country out of the rut. It is only when Jim openly charges him with criminally assaulting his wife that the man behind the mask is revealed. Nimmo's seemingly calm self-restraint, his attempt to transcend personal bitterness and, moreover, his gratitude to Jim and Nina in high sounding terms only exhibit the bland hypocrisy and the lack of correspondence between his words and his action :

> 'My dear fellow, I am not trying to dodge any issue— I am not bluffing. You have been my very understanding

friend, when you allowed me to stay in your house, and Nina to act as my Secretary. You are, in the highest sense of that much abused word, a gentleman. You value true justice—you are not the sport of small considerations, mean gossip and petty jealousies. You despise them, and so does Nina. It is not the least of her virtues, her strong grasp of what really matters in life. Her generous sympathy with old friends—her tolerance, her sense of proportion. You have seen how she has worked for me in the last week of crisis which offers so terrible a threat to all our standards to all we hold dear. I will confess to you that her sympathy, her belief in me at this time when the nation has so unexpectedly—but so decisively and I may say, loudly—called upon me, has been an immense encouragement to me'. (p. 48)

Politics is, for Nimmo, a clever device to sidetrack the moral issue. Persistently booed and scorned by Jim, he quickly changes the topic and tries to impress upon him his indispensability to the country now passing through a crisis :

> The country is tottering on the edge of revolution and you seize this moment to gratify a private spite. At last you see your chance to ruin the man who has never done you anything but kindness—a man over seventy, in any case condemned to die. But you can't wait to dance on my grave and vilify my memory, like all the other jackals who have preyed upon me in life—you are resolved to drag me in the dirt during my last months. And this at the cost of your country. My dear Jim, at least allow yourself to believe that I am not speaking a vain thing. You saw the Press this morning—if not, the papers lie there on the bed. I have some influence still. Say if you like that I have done nothing to deserve this position, but you can't deny or ignore it. Since this last week the whole picture has changed, at this moment my intervention could be decisive. (pp. 66-7)

Later in the novel, Jim catches Nimmo in his wife's bed room. Nimmo at first pretends to be sick and invents an excuse that he fainted and didn't know how he came there. He believes that Jim has seen through his tricks and before Jim raves and strikes at him, he swings to political discourse and leaves his rival stupefied with his verbal gymnastics :

> 'I tell you, Jim, a madhouse. And who is master in this asylum—this raging chaos of pot-bellied union fools and raving paranoiacs. I went to see the P.M. and he had gone to bed. Not to be disturbed on any account. Nor would he see me this morning. That is to say, he dodged. And why', he jumped up, 'why, Jim, why won't he see me ? Because I'd tell him the truth—that the country is slipping into revolution, a revolution it doesn't even want. That nothing can save it now but a national government of all parties. A new government. For this is war. War for the soul of England—the very heart of liberal Europe. And we are ready. Lloyd George will serve. I will serve. In any capacity. We do not demand guarantees, This is not a time for haggling. And always remember this, if we threw in our weight with the workers, we could tell the Tories to get out, we could toss them into the Thames. And make such a revolution the world has never seen—it would transform history—and who would dare to say we were not justified. We have been flouted and ignored—the men who brought this country through the agony of the war—the most tremendous, the most bloody in the history of man. Our experience is despised, by the miserable pettifoggers and time-serveers who are paltering with a crisis equally beyond their imagination and their powers'. (p. 166)

Once in fit of rage Jim hits his wife on the head with a pistol. He repents of his act afterwards and calls for a doctor. Nina refuses to see the doctor and Jim reminds her that she is his wife. In the meantime, Nimmo draws Jim's attention to Nina's qualities and blurts out his own defects. Having seen the perversion in him, it is difficult to adjust oneself to this sober and humble Nimmo who can analyse Nina's character and his own with accuracy and sincerity :

> Nimmo said, 'My dear Jim, let us admit that you and

> I have been at fault to Nina—I—if you like, I will say it—terribly at fault. I do not urge any extenuating circumstances except perhaps that of my old and devoted attachment to the women who was my wife for nearly thirty years and who, in a fit of madness, I divorced. Yet I must urge you to remember that I divorced her, as I thought then, as I think still, for her own happiness. So that at last she could be with the man she had always loved. The one man on earth who could make her completely happy. For I know, Jim—I have known all my life that she did not, could not love me. I was too different in all ways—in mind, in preoccupation, in my very class. Yes, and that goes deep, to the very roots of our grief. I am a cruder, a rougher needed her too much. (p. 61)

Nimmo, entrusted with the task of maintaining law and order in a critical situation arising from the strike, alings himself with the communists who incite the striking workers to violence and endangers the livelihood of three hundred families. Maufe, an honest constable, averts a situation getting worse by arresting Pincomb the communist leader in time and in the scuffle both hit each other. But Nimmo gets Maufe convicted in court and dismisses him from service on charges of assaulting the communist leader, through a conspiracy in which Nina also has part. Shocked by this injustice, Jim tries to kill Nimmo with a razor, but the cunning politician rushes to the lavatory in order to hide himself where he faints and dies. Nimmo's death in a W.C. is a nemesis or the final judgment of Cary for his political sins committed through the years and his lack of moral scruples. John Teeling's comment on Cary's implicit moral judgment on this character is quite pertinent :

> ...the danger in a man like Nimmo who is supremely skilled in both personal and national politics is that he may become the victim of that very skill, and degenerate into a wicked conniving old man.[25]

That is what he became.

---

25. John Teeling, *op. cit.*, p. 283.

Cary had written 'It may be said that all works of art, all ideas of life, all philosophies are "As if" but I am suggesting that they can be checked with an objective reality'.[26] This objective reality can be on different planes, supernatural or natural. As Cary writes : 'When we speak of the novelist and poet's revelation of truth we mean that it is essential moral, that it asserts a moral meaning in the real, and that we can check the meaning by reference to our knowledge of that real. Nimmo's life with its chicanery, cunning and sex is unethical and cannot escape a moral indicement.

Against Nimmo, the political blackguard, Jim stands for honour, justice and truth and seeks to apply these noble principles to the political turmoil of the country reeking in flasehood, shame and the sordid machinations of politics. Jim and Nimmo are characters in contrast. Andrew Wright quotes Cary as referring in the preface to the German edition of *Not Honour More* to the two incompatible temperaments :

> The book shows the clash between two fundamental temperaments and those temperaments are permanent in the world. There are always millions of letters and Nimmos and they will never agree on the ends or even the means of political action.[27]

The novel is full of repeated tirades of Jim against Nimmo and his political duplicity. They sound like paranoic fulminations of a pathological character, but they serve to show the anguished conscience of a bewildered civilian with a sense of morality. He explains why he gave lodging to Nimmo :

> The only reason why this evil man Nimmo was permitted in my house was my life who was under the belief that he was a great man who had saved the country and spent his life in the service of the people. I say he spent his life destroying the country and selling the people. I say he

26. Joyce Cary, *Art and Reality*, p. 20.

27. Andrew Wright, *op. cit.*, p. 149.

> corrupted everything and everybody that came hear him and stole this woman, my wife, from me when she was little more than a child and set to work to destory her body and soul. He wanted her money to get into what he called politics, which was stirring up hatred and envy and making promises he knew would never be fulfilled, and when he caught her he proceed to rob her and terrify her into his slave. I say if a murderer should be hung, which I agree to, them men like Nimmo should be hung twice over because they don't only murder people's bodies but their souls.
>
> I say it's the Nimmo gang who have destroyed all truth and honour in the country, including the sanctity of the home and marriage so that it is nothing but a jobber's match of gimme and what do I get out of it. No confidence or faith in any man and divorces running at fifty thousand a year. (pp. 8-9)

In Jim's book *The Lugas and British African Policy. The Great Betravel,* which he wrote after his dismissal from the African Service, he calls his Lugas better christians than the civilized people of the British government, but he regrets the the corrupting influence of European civilizations :

> England has lost her honour and her soul due to the Whitehall policy of buying off every kind of grapper and smart Alec all over the world by handing over simple tribesmen and helpless poor people to be exploited by so-called nationalists, otherwise local political crooks. (p. 8)

Jim fires three bullets at Nimmo, who escapes unhurt. Nina, who is still inder Nimmo's spell, dislikes it and fears the consequences. Jim sees the police and the reporters and Nina does not how to save the situation. Jim is fearless and bold as he stands for a cause :

> 'The truth', I said, 'Do you think I'm going to play any more of the wangling game ?' For I saw her mind was on the political effects. 'This is something bigger than politics', I said, 'when a man has to defend his home and his honour

> against a conting crook, the lowest of them all. My darling', I said, 'I know I haven't done much good in my life and now I've thrown away my only joy and comfort just when I'd found it again—which is your love and loyality. But at least I've done some good at the end in killing that old swine and stopping some of the rottenness'. (p. 13)

Jim stands for principles and the Rule of Law. He thinks of his crime and law which can be misused :

> The'll call it murder, but what I am out for is truth and justice. I've been a magistrate and I've studies law and I know how important it is to make the law respected, but if the law goes against truth, then it is worse than unless. It is an evil thing because it brings fair dealing and decent conduct into disgust. It brings in the worst corruption because the pople give up all idea of fair dealing and think only of every man looking out for himself. It turns everything into trickery and bluff. (p. 34)

Jim's attempt to murder Nimmo should not lead one to think that he is spiteful against Nimmo on personal grounds. A woman called Brome complains to him that Nimmo had caused the death of her son by sending him off to the war front and wants Jim to take revenge on Nimmo on her behalf. Jim looks at the incident from a public cause :

> For I considered this women a lunatic and best and I wish to make it plain I had no desire at any time to take advantage of this woman's lunatic grievance against Nimmo, not myself acting from any grievance or petty jealousy but in the public interest and decency. (p. 23)

On another occasion he replies to a tall man who calls him a fascist and explains to him that his criticism of Nimmo is not politically motivated :

> This is a foul lie. You know very well I belong to one of the oldest Liberal families in the West and have always been for the people against all oppression. My action

> against Nimmo has nothing to do with politics. It was simply the man is playing a dirty game and leading the country to ruin, including the people. It is too late for politics. (p. 30)

Jim not only exposes the contradictions in Nimmo's character but uses abusive language in his very presence :

> 'You're always talking about morals and all the time you have the lowest idea of how decent ordinary people act. You are always talking about the noble quality of the people and all the time you despise them and wangle them with lies because you think they can't take the truth. You are a man so rotted and soaked in cunning and lies you think everyone is the same. You simply don't know honesty when you see it. You are like a cancer spreading poison everywhere through clean flesh—that's why I say you must be cut out, like a cancer. It's the only way to stop infection spreading'. (p. 49)

For Jim Truth is the Highest ideal to which he is committed. He thus becomes a focal point in the novel, the standard of reality, against which the deflections and the variance of the other characters can be measured. There is an unforgettable passage which shows what Jim stands for :

> My whole case is this, that if a man or country gives up the truth, the absolute truth, they are throwing away the anchor and drifting slowly but surely to destruction. I say nothing can save but truth and the guts to take it. For truth will always prevail. (p. 27)

In order that truth and honour may be vindicated Jim plans to kill his wife whom he loved so dearly for disloyalty and perjury at the Maufe trial. The paradox in his mind finds expression :

> I say I never loved this sweet woman so much as now when I knew she had to die. Because of the rottenness. Because of the corruption. Because all loyalty was a laugh and there was no more trust. (p. 220)

Jim is aware of the truth that the murder of his wife cannot being about an abrupt improvement in the corrupt political atmosphere :

> ...that this great country is so blinded and bound, so hocussed and gammoned by the bunkum boys, the smart ones, the power and money merchants, it doesn't know where it's going or what it's going there for and it's too bewildered to care. (p. 222)

The final sacrifice is a dramatic and poignant scene. Nina, afraid that Jim is going to end her life tries to defend herself. But Jim is determined that she must die as he tells her before the holocaust :

> 'My darling', I said, 'it isn't what you said about me—it's about the fearful thing you and Nimmo have done. Perhaps you think it wasn't very much to betray Maufe and to join in with the liars and cowards and tricksters against an honourable man, against the honour of England. But that only maks it worse—it only proves what I say, that the rottenness has gone too far'. (p. 221)

The time runs out. The deed is done in ritual even as Othello murdered Desdemona ;

> I said we could not wait any more and did she want to pray. She knelt down but said she could not pray, she did not think it would help. But would I forgive her, because she had truly loved me.
>
> I said it was for her to forgive me and I finished the the thing in one stroke. She fell at once and did not struggle at all. (p. 223)

The Duchess in Webster's play *The Duchess of Malfi* knelt down before being strangled to pass through the doors of heaven. Nina kneeling but unable to pray has still in it the nexus of Ultimate Reality and a ruined soul.

Jim awaits execution. This is the end of the Nimmo, Nina Jim affair with which the novel opens :

> This is my statement, so help me God, as I hope to be hung. (p. 5)

Later, towards the end of the novel Jim ruminates :

> They think me mad because I couldn't live like a rat. They think me a fool who murdered the wife he loved for nothing. But it wasn't a murder I did. It was an execution. And I didn't do it for nothing. Not even if the Press have turned it into just another sex crime. I did it because I, myself, had to do it. There was no other choice for man who wasn't prepared to live like a rat. (p. 223)

Jim's love for truth and moral sense have evolved through the same process as described by Cary in *Art and Reality* :

> ...moral sensibility has exactly the same history of development, from the first intuitions of moral feelings and moral action through the education by history, an experience, by religious instruction, to something like a systematic judgment, which is at once rational and emotional.[28]

This novel has two worlds, one private of personal love and marriage, and the other public or the destiny of England for peace and justice after the General Strike. Andrew Wright finds the two worlds merging. He writes, 'in the course of the book the two focuses become one'.[29] According to Robert Bloom 'the two focuses remain two'.[30] The novel deals with the interactableness of life in which Marriage and Politics weave in and out of the story. The Private world and the public world in the complex of the novel are both disjunctive and conjunctive.

In a broadcast on "Unfinished Novels" Cary said once :

> The world is not merely a flux of senseless change. Underneath all the turmoil there are fixed and permanent things.[31]

28. Joyce Cary, *Art and Reality*, p. 154.
29. Andrew Wright, *op. cit.*, p. 151.
30. Robert Bloom, *op. cit.*, p. 171.
31. Quoted by Golden L. Larsen, *op. cit.*, pp, 154-55.

Each character is a 'creative free individual'.[32] At times Cary measures the individual against an avolving system of reality as in *Prisoner of Grace* or a definitive or dogmatic reality as in *Except the Lord.* In *Not Honour More* he deals with three main characters, Jim latter, Nimmo and Nina. They are all shown in juxtaposition to each other. The referential is embodied in a character, Jim Latter, who stands for Honour and justice or ultimate truths. Nimmo and Nina in varying degrees of depravity, can be sized up against Jim's ideal. Even within a single character there can be a pull of opposites of the real and the unreal. Jim's deviation can be estimated from the exis of his goodness—"Loved I not honour more", from Lovelace's poem *To Lucaste, Going to the Wars,* which gave the title to the novel.

32. Robert Bloom, *op. cit.*, p. 197.

Conclusion

Joyce Cary (1888-1957) wrote his first novel *Aissa Saved* in 1932 and *Not Honour More* in 1955, the splendid climax of fifteen novels. His sixteenth *The Captive and the Free*, unfinished, was completed by Winifred Davin, literary Advisor to the estate of Joyce Cary. Even such an original writer, as Cary was, has to be perceptually seen in the tradition of the English novel (Chapter I). He is in the tide of the continuity of the modern novel but, what is truer, in the severance from it, for Cary is inimitable and amazingly Unique. He is a challenging novelist and it takes courage to take up the gauntlet. It was done by three bold critics. The first is Andrew Wright: *Joyce Cary : A Preface to his Novels* (1958) who finds in him the theme of freedom. The second is Robert Bloom : *The Indeterminate World* (1962) who finds in Cary a disquieting indeterminate vision which impairs his novels. The third is Golden Larsen : *The Dark Descent : Social Change and Moral Responsibility in the Novels of Joyce Cary* (1965). The approach is explicit in the sub-title. None of these appear to be centric to Cary's Art and Reality. He ruminated on Reality, Art and the artist and embodied his views in his Clark Lectures published under the title *Art and Reality : Ways of the Creative Process* (1958). Cary's primary purpose was to present the complex of Reality, the stance taken in this thesis.

The first group of four African novels deal with instinctive life and premordial images or primitive reality (Chaptes II). They are within the study of anthropology or dark reality as it appears in primitive consciousness. In *Aissa Saved* (1932) he studies primitive life at the group level. The African characters live in superstition and barbarism. The christian convert

Aissa succumbs to the overpowering and immutable laws of Race. The whole story throbs with jungle fear and foreboding. In An American Visitor (1933) Bewsher, the whiteman, well-intentioned, tries to lift the Birri tribe ; he is martyred by the insensate natives. Marie Hasluck, an anthropologist, is the American visitor, who takes a romantic view of the Birri ; she is soon disillusioned. She marries Bewsher and suffers to see him die. Bewsher's death is differently received by the characters each in the bias of his life. *The African Witch* (1936) is replete with domonology. The African native Aladai, educated at Oxford, is subdued by his sister Elizabeth the priestess with magical powers. The *juju* spirit is symbolized in that creature of terror, the crocodile. In *Mister Johnson* (1939), a youth of seventeen is obsessed with civilized life. He takes part in the building of a road which stands as a symbol of Western progress. Johnson helps Rudbeck, but is caught in crime. He is sentenced to death but before that takes place Rudbeck shoorts him. All four African novels, with their own slants of truth, deal with primitive reality.

In the two novels *Charley is My Darling* (1940) and *A House of Children* (1941) Cary is concerned with imaginative reality (Chapter III). The child is in a continuous process of building an ordered world from the fragmentary. In *Charley is My Darling* crime is considered as a moral experiment. The story is one of adjustment and disaster. The novel *A House of Children* is written with lyrical fervour. It gives a romantic view of childhood with its mingling of the sensory and the imaginative.

The first trilogy presents human reality (Chapter IV). The three novels with the chaos of life and the universal within it. In *Herself Surprised* (1941) Sara, the broken woman, turns on herself to the goodness that could be possible but which was not hers. In *To be a Pilgrim* (1942) we are shown three generations. The characters form two groups, the aberrants and the constants, those in the unreal and those in the real. *The Horse's Mouth* (1944) is the last novel of the group. It deals with the life of Sulley Jimson, the wayward artist, whose *The Fall* is put to rude use for patching the roof of Mrs. Coker and *The Crea-*

tion in the drawing of which Gulley Jimson suffers a fall. This comedy is a triumph of laughter, what happens to a soldier, just before he goes out to no-man's land and death.

Dogmatic Reality (Chapter V) is of two kinds—that which is based on a system of sanctioned dogmas in a religion and that which is privately evolved. As the first deals with the transcendental and Absolute Reality, outside the mind, the second deals with Relative Reality. *Prisoner of Grace* (1952) is shown as dealing with the relativism of dogmatic Reality, *Except the Lord* (1953) with moral absolutism or dogma in Evangelical christianity and *Not Honour More* (1955) with the ultimate perceived by the character, Jim Latter in particular moments of his life.

The works of Joyce Cary moves from intuition to concept. Each novel is occasioned by an intuition or a discovery, or an impression or some passing thought usually expressed in the Prefatory Essay of the novel where on such exists. As the novel evolves and human beings work out their destinies as free souls, they find themselves facing the changeless and the permanent. All works of art, once wrote Cary, 'exist and must exist within a universal moral real' (*Art and Reality*, p. 169). This is the Reality, multiform in its very nature, which Cary dissects and presents, in striking differentiation and selective proportions, Cary's 'Compositional scale of fiction' is appropriate to the complexity of life' (Possibilities Essays on the state of the Novel by Malcolm Bradbury, p. 277). To explain and expound the novels from this point of view has been the burden of this thesis.

Bibliography

(1) SELECT ORIGINAL WORKS

Aissa Saved. Carfax Edition, Michael Joseph, London, Reprinted 1960.

An American Visitor. Carfax Edition, Michael Joseph, London, Reprinted 1960.

An African Witch. Carfax Edition, Michael Joseph, London, Reprinted 1961.

Mister Johnson. Carfax Edition, Michael Joseph, London, Reprinted 1961.

Charley is My Darling. Carfax Edition, Michael Joseph, London, Reprinted 1961.

A House of Children, Carfax Edition, Michael Joseph, London, Reprinted 1961.

Herself Surprised. Carfax Edition, Michael Joseph, London, Reprinted 1960.

To Be a Pilgrim. Carfax Edition, Michael Joseph, London, Reprinted 1959.

The Hourse's Mouth. Carfax Edition, Michael Joseph, London, Reprinted 1959.

Prisoner of Grace. Carfax Edition, Michael Joseph, London, Reprinted 1960.

Except the Lord. Michael Joseph, London, 1953.

Not Honour More. Michael Joseph, London, 1955.

Art and Reality. Anchor Books Doubleday & Co., New York, 1961.

(2) CRITICISM ON CARY

Allen, Walter, *Joyce Cary* (Revised), The British Council, Longmans, Green & Co., London, 1963.

Bloom, Robert, *The Indeterminate World: A Study of the Novels of Joyce Cary,* University of Pennsyivania Press, Philadelphia, 1962.

Larsen, Golden L., *The Dark Descent : Social Change and Moral Responsibility in the Novels of Joyce Cary,* Michael Joseph, London, 1965.

Wright, Andrew, *Joyce Cary : A Preface to his Novels,* Chatto and Windus, London, 1959.

(3) STUDIES ON THE NOVEL

Allen, Walter, *The English Novel,* Penguin Books, Reprinted 1963.

——, *Tradition and Dream,* Penguin Books, 1965.

Beach, Joseph Warren, *English Literature of the 19th and the early 20th Centuries, 1798 to the First World War,* Collier Books, New York, 1962.

Booth, Wayne C., *The Rhetoric of Fiction,* The University of Chicago Press, Chicago, 1961.

Bradbury, Malcolm, *Possibilities,* Essays on the State of the Novel, Oxford University Press, 1973.

Cecil, David, *Early Victorian Novelists,* Constable & Co. Ltd., London, 1935.

Drew, Elizabeth, *A Modern Guide to Fifteen English Masterpieces,* A Laurel Edition, New York, 1963.

Forster, E.M., *Aspects of the Novel,* Penguin Books, 1963.

Hardy, Barbara, *The Appropriate Form*, University of London, The Athlone Press, 1964.

Humphrey, Robert, *Stream of Consciousness in the Modern Novel*, University of California Press, Berkely, 1954.

Karl, Frederick R., *A Reader's Guide to the Contemporary English Novel*, Thames and Hudson, London, 1963.

Kettle, Arnold, *An Introduction to the English Novel*, Vol. II, Arrow Books Ltd., London, 1962.

Knecht, Edward Wagen, *Cavalcade of the English Novel*, Holt, Rinehart and Winston, New York, 1954.

Knoepffmacher, U.C., *Religious Humanism and the Victorian Novel*, Princeton University Press, New Jersey, 1965.

Leavis, F.R., *The Great Tradition*, Penguin Books, 1962.

Loofbourow, John, *Thackeray and the Form of Fiction*, Princeton University Press, Princeton, New Jersey, 1964.

McCormick, John, *Catastrophe and Imagination*, Longmans, Green & Co., London, 1957.

Muir, Edwin, *The Structure of the Novel*, The Hogarth Press, London, 1960.

O'Cornor, William Van., ed., *Forms of Modern Fiction*, Indian a University Press, Bloomington, 1961.

O'Faolain, Sean, The Vanishing Hero, Eyre and Spottiswoode, London, 1956.

Prescott, Orville, *In My Opinion : An Inquiry into the Contemporary Novel*, New York, 1952.

Schorer, Mark, ed., *Modern British Fiction*, Oxford University Press, New York, 1961.

West, Paul, *The Modern Novel*, Vol. I and II, Hutchinson University Library, London, 1965.

(4) NOVELS

Defoe, Daniel, *Moll Flanders*, Boston, 1903.

Greene, Graham, *The Heart of the Matter*, London, 1948.

Hemingway, Ernest, *A Farewell to Arms*, Penguin Books, 1955.

Huxley, Aldous, *Point Counter Point*, Penguin Books, Reprinted 1965.

——, *Those Barren Leaves*, Penguin Books, Reprinted 1961.

——, *The Genuis and the Goddess*, London, 1955.

Newman, John Henry, *Loss and Gain*, Burns, Oates & Co., London, 1876.

(5) GENERAL

Sakar, Herschel, *The Dignity of Man*, Harvard University Press, 1947.

Baldwin, Alfred L., *Behaviour and Development in Childhood*, The Dryden Press, New York, 1956.

Breckenridge, Marien E. and Vincent, E ; Lee, Child Development, W.B. Saunders Company, Philadelphia, 1960.

Cloward, Richard A. and Ohlin, Lloyd E., *Delinquency and Opportunity, A Theory of Delinquent Gangs*, The Free Press of Glencoe, New York, 1960.

Cowley, Malcolm., ed., *The Writer at Work : The Paris Review Interviews*, New York : Viking, 1958.

Crow, Laster D. and Crow, Alice, *Adolescent Development and Adjustment*, McGraw-Hill Book Company, New York, 1956.

Edel, Leon, ed., *The House of Fiction*, Mercury Books, London, 1962.

English Critical Essay—Twentieth Century, The World's Classies, Oxford University Press, London, 1958.

Everett, Millard Spencer, *Ideals of Life*, John Willey & Sons, New York, 1954.

Frazer, Sir James George, *The Golden Bough*, Macmillan & Cp., Ltd., London, 1955.

Huxley, Aldous., ed., *Letters of D.H. Lawrence*, William Heinemann Ltd., London, 1952.

Jersild, Arthur T., *The Psychology of Adolescence*, The Macmillan Company, New York, 1957.

Joad, C.E.M., *Guide to the Philosophy of Morals and Politics*, Victor Gollancz Ltd., London, 1938.

Laird, John, *On Human Freedom*, George Allen & Unwin Ltd., London, 1947.

Lamont, W.D., *The Principles of Moral Judgment*, Clarendon Press, Oxford, 1946.

Lawrence, D.H., *Fantasia of the Unconscious*.

——, *Twilight in Italy*.

Leeuw, G. Van Der, *Religion in Essence and Manifestation*, tr. Turner, J.E. George Allen and Unwin Ltd., London, 1938.

Morgan, Arthur E., *Search for Purpose*, The Antioch Press, Ohio, 1955.

Nuys, Kelvin Van, *Science and Cosmic Purpose*, Rider and Company, London, 1951.

Potts, L.J., *Comedy*, Hutchinson's University Library, London, 1948.

Richardson, Joanna, ed., *Essays by Divers Hands*, Jew Series, Oxford University Press, London, 1963.

Schilder, Paul, *Mind : Perception and Thought in their Constructive Aspects*, Columbia University Press, New York, 1942.

Shapira, Morris, ed., *Henry James : Collected Literary Criticism*, Heinemann, London, 1963.

Scheldon, Wilmon Henry, *God and Polarity*, Yale University Press, New York, 1954.

Skinner, Charles E. and Harriman, Philip Laurence, ed., Child Psychology, The Macmillan Company, New York, 1960.

Woolf, Virginia, A., Writer's Diary, ed., Woolf, Leonard, Hogarth Press, London, 1953.

(6) JOURNALS

Antioch Review, XVII, Summer 1957.

Dalhousie Review, XXXVIII, Winter 1959.

Modern Fiction Studies, IX, No. 3, Autumn 1963.

New State and Nation, October 27, 1951.

Paris Review, VIII, Winter 1954-55.

Partison Review, XXXII, No. 2, Spring 1966.

Tamarack Review, No. 10, Winter 1959.

Taxes Studies in Literature and Language, II, Autumn 1960.

University of Toronto Quarterly, XXIX, No. 3, April 1960.

Western Humanities Review, XIII, No. 2, Spring 1959.